HISTORIC TALES *of*

BETHEL

CONNECTICUT

Best Wishes,

Patick Wild

HISTORIC TALES *of*

BETHEL

CONNECTICUT

Patrick Tierney Wild

Charleston  London

THE
History
PRESS

Published by The History Press
Charleston, SC 29403
www.historypress.net

Images are courtesy of the author unless otherwise noted.

First published 2011

Manufactured in the United States

ISBN 978.1.60949.357.8

Library of Congress Cataloging-in-Publication Data

Wild, Patrick Tierney.
Historic tales of Bethel, Connecticut / Patrick Tierney Wild.
p. cm.
Includes bibliographical references.
ISBN 978-1-60949-357-8
1. Bethel (Conn. : Town)--History. 2. Bethel (Conn. : Town)--Biography. I. Title.
F104.B46 W56
974.6'9--dc23
2011037321

For my mother,

Jean V. Wild,

who always encouraged my love of books

Contents

CONTENTS

Acknowledgements

Writing even a small book such as this one can be a daunting task. No one who has ever engaged in extensive historical research could truthfully claim to work alone. Accessing historical records and gaining firsthand accounts are the lifeblood of investigating the past, and no one has unlimited information within reach of his fingertips, even with today's Internet. This book, then, is truly not the work of any one person but rather of a collection of people who all contributed key ingredients. Therefore, those individuals and groups who played a vital role in the creation of this book should rightfully be recognized.

First and foremost, I wish to thank the dedicated staff of the Danbury Museum and Historical Society: Bridget Guertin, Levi Newsome, Robert Young and most of all, Diane Hassan. They do a remarkable job of preserving historical artifacts and information related to the Danbury area's past. They are always welcoming and friendly and were exceedingly helpful. The service they render to the community cannot be quantified, and I am greatly appreciative for their assistance in obtaining key photographs and for permitting me to examine newspapers and documents that were of vital importance in tracing the story of Bethel's past.

The employees of the Bethel town clerk's office, town clerk Lisa Bergh, as well as Carol Ritch and Ellen Jelinski, were always tremendously accommodating in allowing me to search old records within the confines of the town vault. They serve the town of Bethel well and should never be overlooked for the great work they do in assisting so many.

The staff of the Bethel Public Library, Danbury Public Library and the Cyrenius H. Booth Library in Newtown all proved very efficient on those times I visited them to research. The Connecticut State Library is also to be thanked for allowing images from the Clark Photograph Collection to be utilized for this book. My gratitude goes out to Edith K. Meffley, Ruth Stevenson MacGill, Judith Allison Walters and the Goodsell family for the information they provided on the Plumtrees Schoolhouse. Thanks are expressed to the Bethel Historical Society for the many times over the years that I have been permitted to examine their holdings for background information. Their collection is a treasure-trove for lovers of our town's past. Historian and genealogist Gary Boughton provided assistance in his transcription of notes left by Henry B. Betts on Stony Hill that made the research process a great deal easier.

My brother James H. Wild III and sister Cathleen M. Durkee provided more help than they know in researching the Plumtrees Schoolhouse. My brother provided his architectural observations and views regarding the building's construction, while my sister shared many memories of her days as a student there and of her wonderfully kind and caring third grade teacher, Miss Edith Cushnie (now Mrs. Edith Weighart). Jeff Saraceno, commissioning editor, and Jaime Muehl, senior editor, of The History Press were remarkable in their efforts to guide me through the publication process and in helping to ensure that this book was assembled in a quality manner.

An enormous expression of thanks goes to my patient and tolerant family who showed understanding throughout the time it took to complete this book. My wife, Alexa, has a remarkable knowledge of English grammar, and her assistance in reading over my work was invaluable. My son Jonathan and daughter Rebecca also contributed assistance by their continual expression of interest and encouragement throughout the project.

Finally, I wish to express gratitude to my mother, Mrs. Jean V. Wild, and my late father, James H. Wild Jr., for providing me the opportunity of growing up in Bethel. My appreciation of that experience increases with each passing day.

Introduction

In January 1988, I moved into a first-floor apartment of a historic home then owned by my brother Jim at 16 Main Street in Bethel. Little did I know how the home would influence me in the coming years. My brother had always been interested in the history of the house and had done a good deal of research since purchasing it in 1973. As a way of expressing my gratitude to my brother for being allowed to rent the home, I decided that I would do some further historical research on the house to help fill in any missing pieces in its history. In the course of my investigations I delved into land records held by both the town of Bethel and the city of Danbury. After a while, I had pretty much pieced together the complete string of owners dating from 1790 to 1988. Still feeling the need to get a fuller picture, I began researching the ownership of neighboring houses until I became acquainted with most of Main Street. Not satisfied with that, I then began going to the library to examine local histories to learn more about early Bethel and to see if any of the homeowners had been individuals of prominence. I visited the Scott-Fanton Museum in Danbury (now the Danbury Museum and Historical Society) to become acquainted with historic maps of the area, as well as newspapers that carried accounts of local events over time. Before I knew it, I was hooked. The town's history had become my new obsession, and in 1993 I was officially appointed Bethel's first town historian.

In searching for information related to Bethel's history, I found that there was not as much published information as I had anticipated, and what was available was scant on specifics or in many cases borrowed liberally from earlier works. The starting point for anyone interested in the history of Bethel would undoubtedly have to be the *History of Danbury, Conn. 1684–1896* by James Montgomery Bailey. Owing to the fact that Bethel remained part of Danbury until 1855, this work is the logical beginning for acquainting one's self with the early history of the area. The book also devotes its final chapter of true text specifically to Bethel. Another ancient tome worth consulting is the *Commemorative Biographical Record of Fairfield County, Connecticut* published by J.H. Beers and Company in 1899. It contains biographies and portraits of prominent individuals from the turn of the century, as well as their family histories, and includes a great deal of detailed information not found elsewhere. Another hefty volume of interest also from the Gilded Age is the *History of Fairfield County, Connecticut* compiled by D. Hamilton Hurd in 1881. This work contains a brief history of the town written by Dr. George Benedict, whose family was one of the first to settle in the Danbury/Bethel area. The history focuses on commercial, ecclesiastical, political and military data, as well as providing a pair of short biographical sketches of two prominent hat manufacturers of the time. *Four Cities and Towns of Connecticut,* produced in 1890 by the Acme Publishing and Engraving Company of New York, provides eight separate accounts of prominent manufacturers and companies found in Bethel at that time period.

A book prepared as part of Bethel's centennial celebration in 1955 is also of considerable value. Simply entitled *Bethel Connecticut Centennial, 1855–1955,* this paperback contains essays written by Lewis E. Goodsell, Ernest E. Miller, Katharine La Valla and Burton F. Sherwood, among others. The work also contains many unique photographs worthy of note. *The History of a Yankee Church* by Lewis Goodsell that was first published in 1960 and revised in 1976 focuses on the history of the town's Congregational Church but has much information that is also integral to the town's past. For the nation's bicentennial in 1976, the Bethel Historical Society published *A History of Bethel 1759–1976.* Much of this book is a reprint of the 1955 centennial book but also includes new material of merit, including a section on historic houses, many of which have been demolished in the last thirty-five years.

There are also smaller pamphlets, booklets and short sections of larger works that prove useful. John Warner Barber's *Historical Collections of Connecticut*, published in 1836, contains a short section on Bethel. Another resource is a small paperback entitled *Connecticut Tercentenary Celebration Danbury-Bethel* published in 1935 by the Tercentenary Committee composed of individuals from both towns. Also published in 1935 is *The Connecticut Guide, What To See and Where To Find It* compiled by Edgar L. Heermance and published by the Emergency Relief Commission. This work has descriptions of historic points of interests for all Connecticut towns, including Bethel. Produced in 1937, the *Guide to the History and the Historic Sites of Connecticut* written by Florence S. Marcy Crofut and published by the Yale University Press contains two pages of content relating to Bethel. A short book entitled *History of Ye Old Town Hall* produced by the Bethel Veterans of Foreign Wars in 1950 has both information and photographs that are of use. The book was only produced in small numbers but is available at the Bethel Public Library. The 1955 *Price and Lee City Directory for Danbury and Bethel* contains a brief but informative history of Bethel found on pages 786 to 794. One work that is especially well researched is entitled *History of Bethel, Connecticut: An Excerpt from Plan of Development Bethel, Connecticut*, which was written by Edward J. Gallagher and published by Technical Planning Associates in 1969. Incorporated as one section of a larger plan of development book, this nineteen-page account is both original and thorough, given its length.

All of these works, as well as Danbury newspapers that over time have included *The Farmer's Journal*, the *Danbury Recorder*, the *Danbury Gazette*, the *Danbury Times*, the *Danbury Democrat*, the *Jeffersonian*, the *Danbury News*, the *Danbury Evening News* and the *Danbury News-Times*, have been examined for this book. Bethel newspapers consulted include P.T. Barnum's own *Herald of Freedom* and later *Herald of Freedom and Gospel Witness*, as well as scattered copies of others such as the *Bethel Press*, the *Bethel Ledger*, the *Bethel Eagle*, the *Bethel Sunbeam*, the *Bethel News*, the *Bethel Home News*, the *Bethel Beacon*, the *Valley Ledger* and one paper from the 1880s with the bizarre title of the *Yellow Spasm*.

The aim of this book is not to relate a comprehensive history of the town but rather to share a collection of historical vignettes that will hopefully familiarize the reader with aspects of the town not widely recognized. These short stories tell much about the development of the town and the character of the individuals who developed it. Many of them first appeared as articles in the *Bethel Home News* or *Bethel Beacon* before their discontinuation. Most of the previously published pieces have been updated and revised and appear together in book form for the very first time.

Having spent the last half century in Bethel, I have seen it change enormously. In 1960, the population of Bethel was 8,200 people. When the census was taken in 2010, the population had reached 18,584. This addition of 10,384 individuals may seem inconsequential to larger communities, but to a town composed of only seventeen square miles, the increase was earthshaking to say the least. In looking back over the town's past, I have discovered that it has experienced many other population surges over time, but none quite as dramatic as that experienced from 1950 to 1970. Like all towns, Bethel has had good times and bad and has made some sound decisions and some questionable ones that have helped to determine its current status. Other changes have been brought about by forces outside the town's control. The demise of the hatting industry, the abandonment of small farming, the proliferation of strip shopping centers and the construction of a nearby interstate highway have all had deep impacts on the town and transformed its very nature. Despite these seismic changes, Bethel continues to grow and thrive and will hopefully proceed along that same path in a positive way, far into the future.

Among the more cherished memories of a life spent in Bethel are such things as attending kindergarten at the Plumtrees one-room schoolhouse, going to the 4-H Fair in Stony Hill and the Apple Blossom Festival at Blue Jay Orchards, shopping at Jerome's five-and-ten-cent store, buying candy at Mullaney's store, and acquiring my St. Mary's School uniform at Noe's clothing store. I remember with great fondness delivering the *Danbury News-Times* on my bicycle before newspaper boys were replaced by paper "carriers," otherwise known as adults in automobiles. I remember milk being delivered by the milkman from Marcus Dairy at five o'clock in the morning and the streets being oiled and sanded each summer to keep them in good repair. Sledding on snow-covered roads and skating on ice-laden ponds were then an important part of growing up in Bethel. It is my sincere wish that the children of this generation and of many generations to come will treasure their childhood years spent in Bethel with equal fondness.

1
The Legend of
Luther Holcomb

Bethel's Revolutionary Riddle

There is a passage in John Warner Barber's *Historical Collections of Connecticut* published in 1836 that is especially intriguing to those interested in Bethel history. It concerns an incident that occurred on what is today Route 58 or Putnam Park Road near the eastern side of Hoyt's Hill on that fateful day when the British invaded Danbury: April 26, 1777. The passage reads as follows:

> As the British were descending the hill, a short distance from the village, on the old Reading road, one of the inhabitants of the town, Mr. Luther Holcomb, rode his horse up to the summit of an eminence in front of the enemy. Although entirely alone, Mr. Holcomb, (judging from the words he used), evidently intended to make an impression. Waving his hat or sword, and turning his face as though he was addressing an army behind him, he exclaimed in a voice of thunder, "Halt the whole Universe! Break off by kingdoms!" This, it must be confessed, was a formidable force to encounter. The British came to a halt, their cannon were brought forward and made to bear upon their supposed opponents, and flanking parties sent out to make discoveries. Mr. Holcomb, on the point of being surrounded, and deeming discretion the better part of valor, thought it advisable to make good his retreat in a rapid manner towards Danbury.

Upon first reading this account, one might quickly ask the meaning of the words that this seemingly deranged antagonist shouted to his imaginary forces. A modern translation might be, "Everyone Stop! Divide yourselves up by the nations you represent!" Obviously, this Connecticut Yankee was laying it on a bit thick.

A second question that comes to mind might be to ask just what this eccentric individual was attempting to accomplish by his theatrics. Although the true motivation may have been known only to Holcomb, there is a good possibility that this unique show of bravado was an attempt to stall the King's forces long enough to allow a greater number of Danbury's citizens to flee their homes and cart off their endangered valuables.

If this was the case, and Holcomb was indeed risking his life to aid his fellow townsmen, then he unquestionably qualifies as a minor hero in the American attempt to thwart General William Tryon's invading forces. But was there ever an individual named Luther Holcomb living in the Bethel parish of Danbury at the time of the Revolution, or is this just another fanciful yarn dreamed up by some mischievous "Nutmegger" in 1834 in order to get John Warner Barber's literary goat? More succinctly, was Luther Holcomb fact or fiction?

This incident, first described by Barber in 1836, has often been repeated. Variations on this account have appeared in Henry C. Deming's *Oration on the Life and Services of General David Wooster* in 1854, Gideon Hiram Hollister's *History of Connecticut* in 1855, Benson J. Lossing's *Pictorial Field-Book of the Revolution* in 1860 and James Montgomery Bailey's *History of Danbury* in 1896. Deming was the first to identify the site of Holcomb's encounter with the British as being Hoyt's Hill in Bethel. Bailey identifies Holcomb solely as "a presumably insane horseman."

But perhaps the most interesting version of the tale can be found in a Holcomb family genealogy written by Elizabeth Weir McPherson in 1947 with the ponderous title of *The Holcombes, nation builders: a family having as great a part as any in the making of all North American civilization, their biographies, genealogies and pedigrees*. Its interpretation is singular to say the least:

> *Luther Holcomb was a resident of Danbury, Fairfield Co., Conn. during the American Revolution and was familiar with the locations in which the adjoining and neighboring hills best gave back in echoes sounds sent against them. He so concealed himself there and so used his rare talents of mimicry*

Artist and writer John Warner Barber's engraving of Bethel based on a sketch completed in September 1834. The scene depicted is lower Chestnut Street with Main Street branching off to the left and Maple Avenue branching to the right. The church shown in the center of the image is the first Congregational meetinghouse, which was constructed in 1760 and destroyed by fire on July 21, 1842. The three houses shown farthest to the right all survive to the present day.

and ventriloquism in calling conflicting and confusing commands to 3,000 British invaders marching through Danbury from Bethel. This slowed the march a considerable time. During the confusion Luther escaped.

This edition of the tale seems the most dubious and is made even less credible by its exaggeration of the British force by roughly twelve hundred men.

It is clear that there was indeed a Luther Holcomb residing in Bethel parish during Revolutionary times. Land records show that he lived in a relatively small house that was later incorporated into a larger one, now labeled as 45 Greenwood Avenue—a location, incidentally, that is located diagonally across from the base of Hoyt's Hill. Holcomb's name appears on the Danbury tax lists, land records and vital statistics. His name also appears within the pages of Danbury's first newspaper, *The Farmer's Journal*, and those of the records of the Bethel Congregational Church, where it is noted that at one point Holcomb was given the job of sweeping the meetinghouse and shutting the doors and windows.

The most detailed information concerning Holcomb's life comes predominately from two sources: the aforementioned *The Holcombes* and Holcomb's military pension application of 1832. According to these sources, Luther Holcomb was born on August 12, 1752, in the parish of Wintonbury in Old Windsor (now Bloomfield), Connecticut, the eighth child of Matthew Holcomb and Lydia (Drake) Holcomb. (Consequently, Holcomb would have been a few months shy of his twenty-fifth birthday at the time of the British raid.) In adulthood, Holcomb moved to the Bethel parish of Danbury and married Judith Beebe, the second daughter of Lemuel and Hannah (Dibble) Beebe of Bethel. His father-in-law, Lemuel Beebe, operated a mill on Plumtrees Brook not far from the present site of the Plumtrees Schoolhouse. He would go on to marry twice more, marrying Johannah Kellog of Danbury in 1784 and Sally Newton of Bainbridge, New York, in 1819. Over the course of his three marriages, Holcomb fathered thirteen children. Holcomb left the Danbury area about the year 1797 judging by the last time he sold land as recorded in the Danbury land records. He then took up residence in Winchester, Litchfield County, Connecticut. While there he was chosen to serve as a presidential elector. *The Holcombes* relates the interesting anecdote that "Old Luther Holcomb often appeared in public carrying his violin from his shoulder. One Oliver Smith, an exhorter, of Southwick Hampden Co., Mass. was so enraged at the public display of Luther's 'fiddle' that he smashed it. For this Luther sued him." About the year 1805, he moved to Coventry, Chenango County, New York. He was appointed one of the town's fence viewers on March 4, 1806. He died in Coventry on June 22, 1839, at the age of eighty-seven. His grave is flanked by those of two of his wives in the small North Afton Cemetery in the town of Afton, New York—a place I had the opportunity to visit in July 1991.

These are the specifics of Holcomb's life, but the more colorful details are found in his application for a military pension dated August 13, 1832. Here we find no mention of the incident on Hoyt's Hill, but what we do find suggests that Holcomb was an ardent Patriot who was actively involved in America's drive for independence. Holcomb testified under oath at the time of his pension application that he had first enlisted at Danbury in December 1775 for the term of three months in the company of Captain Noble Benedict, serving under Lieutenant John Trowbridge and Ensign James Clark in a regiment commanded by Colonel Return J. Meigs.

The Legend of Luther Holcomb

According to Holcomb, over the course of the next two years, and in various military units, he participated at "the retreat out of New York at the time they [the American troops] were blocked by the British troops—The Battle of Ridgebury [actually Ridgefield] where General [Benedict] Arnold's horse was shot under him—an engagement at Compo Hill in Conn [a skirmish that took place in Westport as the British tried to embark after their destruction of Danbury],—in two general Battles at the taking of Burgoyne [the Battles of Saratoga, New York, in September and October 1777, which most historians view as the turning point of the Revolution]." During this last engagement, Holcomb states that he "received a slight wound."

During January 1777, Holcomb enlisted as an artificer (skilled workman) in Danbury under the command of David Wood. His occupation was that of a wagon maker. He continued in this work, when not called away to fight, "for a term of two years and nine months, at which time he became disabled from a wound in his knee by an adze." Thus, Holcomb's official service position might have been that of artificer at the time of the Danbury raid. It is ironic to note that over two and a quarter centuries later he would be most remembered for employing a very different form of artifice.

The most mysterious part of the Luther Holcomb story is that there is no documented record of his having served in the war. He was ultimately denied his pension because he received no written discharge and also because he failed to furnish proof of service of six months as required by the pension laws. However, in his application, he was able to furnish specific military activities in detail and provide the names of those with whom he served, such as Benjamin Hickok, Noble Benedict, General Gold Selleck Silliman and other known veterans. It seems unlikely that Holcomb would have been able to supply such detailed information had he not seen at least some military service.

Thus, in searching Holcomb's pension application for proof of his halting the British on Hoyt's Hill, no such proof was found. This does not necessarily mean the incident did not take place. The first teller of this tale, John Warner Barber, reportedly enhanced his "historical collections" of each town with anecdotes provided by local residents. This may be the manner in which this story was first recorded. At the time of Barber's visit to Danbury in September 1834, many townspeople who would have known Holcomb personally were still living. (Holcomb himself, though residing in New York,

The tombstone in the center of this photo marks the grave of Luther Holcomb. A variety of accounts, written years after the American Revolution, suggest that Holcomb used uniquely deceptive methods to delay British forces on their way to capture military stores kept in Danbury. Holcomb later moved to New York State and was laid to rest in the North Afton Cemetery located in Afton, New York, not far from the city of Binghamton.

was also still alive and would be for another five years.) Even a century after the American Revolution, P.T. Barnum, who was born in 1810, would state how his uncles, aunts and others "remembered and described the burning of Danbury by the British." Although the authenticity of Luther Holcomb's stand at Hoyt's Hill cannot be definitively documented, there is much to suggest that he did stand with those who risked everything they had in order to trade tyranny for democracy, and for that alone he should be considered a hero worth remembering.

2

Captain Daniel Hickok and the Night of the Three Generals

Daniel Hickok may have been a simple cobbler, but he was a man of action. When his fledgling nation called in 1775, he answered. His story is one that typifies the life of a New England Revolutionary War Patriot. His home at 13 Blackman Avenue survives to this day, to remind us that many great heroes of America's War of Independence are not mentioned in our history textbooks.

The Hickok family was one of the earliest to settle in what would eventually become Bethel. Various land and probate records indicate that Daniel Hickok's father, Ebenezer, seems to have migrated from his birthplace in Waterbury to the Danbury area in the 1720s. He obviously owned a considerable amount of land in Bethel as shown by the distribution of his estate following his death on July 8, 1774. The elder Hickok and his second wife, Esther, had been two of the seventy-one original members of the Congregational Church established in 1759. Church records show that Ebenezer Hickok served as deacon from as early as 1760 up until the time of his death, and it was Hickok who donated "the land for a burying ground, and a site for a meeting house."

Daniel Hickok, born in Bethel in 1748, was the fourth child in a family of seven who had been produced by his father's two marriages. In May 1775, only a few weeks after the Battle of Lexington and Concord, which initiated the American Revolution, the twenty-seven-year-old Hickok "received an ensign's commission from the Governor of Connecticut with an order to enlist men for service of the states." Hickok's 1832 pension application, on file at the National Archives in Washington, tells the story of his military service in his own words: "I soon had orders to march the company commanded by Capt. Noble Benedict to the northward as far as Ticonderoga where I served on this tour seven months. Early in January 1776 the regiment to which I belonged was ordered to New York & I accordingly marched with my company to New York where I was in service two months & a half." In the spring of 1776, Hickok was appointed captain of a local militia.

Hickok's pension application goes on to chronicle his later military service: "In the year 1777 I was ordered out with my company near the Hudson River and marched there as far north as Red-hook on said River at this time I was in service one month and a half. Soon after my return from Red-hook I was again called out with my company towards New York and marched to a place called Sawpits & was at this time in service two months." Hickok went on to serve under Colonel David Humphreys at "the seaboard" and under Israel Putnam at Peekskill, New York.

Of all the military service seen by Hickok, the one of greatest local interest would be that which occurred in April 1777. On the morning of the twenty-sixth of that month, a British expeditionary force led by Brigadier General William Tryon, consisting of approximately eighteen hundred British troops, left their ships in Westport and began a march toward Danbury to destroy the large repository of military supplies that had been placed there. As word spread of the invasion, all available Continental troops and local militias were collected in an effort to thwart the British attack. The leaders in this effort would be Brigadier General David Wooster, Brigadier General Gold Selleck Silliman and none other than Brigadier General Benedict Arnold. These three officers rendezvoused at Redding and were able to assemble a combined force of approximately six hundred men. By the time this force reached as far as Bethel on that Saturday night of April 26, 1777, it was nearly 11:30 p.m. A driving rain had made their march miserable and their guns useless. With the British already stationed in Danbury's center, it was decided that the colonial forces should encamp overnight in Bethel and arise early in the morning to attack the enemy on its anticipated return along the same course it had taken en route to its objective. (It is wondered whether General Silliman stopped for any time at the house of his brother Ebenezer, atop Hoyt's Hill.)

Captain Daniel Hickok and the Night of the Three Generals

This image of the Daniel Hickok House, located at 13 Blackman Avenue, first appeared in Bailey's *History of Danbury* in 1896. Local legend and at least one old record suggest that Generals Benedict Arnold, David Wooster and Gold Selleck Silliman may have spent the night here on April 26, 1777.

According to local legend, when the three American generals—Wooster, Silliman and Arnold—sought shelter from the torrential downpour that night, they chose the home of Captain Daniel Hickok. There is no concrete evidence available that would verify this event, but according to a work published in 1889 entitled *Record of Connecticut Men in the War of the Revolution...*, Captain Daniel Hickok was "with Wooster in the early spring of '77." This being the case, it would seem plausible that the officers would find shelter with a captain who lived in Bethel and who had knowledge of the area's topography that could assist in the battle plans for the following morning.

It would have been quite a night for the Hickok family. Hickok's twenty-seven-year-old wife, Lucy, was two months pregnant with her fourth child, and her existing children—Daniel Jr., six; Esther, five; and Noah, two—would have had a difficult time sleeping with all the commotion caused by the arrival of their illustrious guests. The generals were awake past 2:00 a.m. plotting their strategy, but by later that same morning, word came that their initial plan to await the return of the British along their original route would now have to be scrapped. It was discovered that the expected foes had set fire to Danbury during the night and were escaping via Ridgefield to avoid being slowed by confrontation with the colonial forces. It would be in Ridgefield, rather than Bethel, that the three generals would see combat. For General Wooster the battle would bring death; General Silliman would survive but would be captured by the British later that same year; and although he was remembered as the hero of the Battle of Ridgefield, and would prove his heroism again six months later at the decisive Battle of Saratoga, Benedict Arnold's eventual shift of loyalties would make his name forever synonymous with treachery.

After the war, Daniel Hickok would return to his business of shoemaking. His wife, Lucy, died in April 1795 at the age of forty-six. He would marry again shortly thereafter, this time to a wealthy widow named Mercy Comstock, who had four children of her own. There must have been difficulty in accommodating everyone in the confines of their saltbox-style home on those occasions when the entire family was all together at once. In 1832, the aging captain would begin to receive his much sought-after military pension.

Daniel Hickok lived to the ripe old age of eighty-eight and died on Christmas Eve 1835. P.T. Barnum would recall nearly fifty years later, "In Old Lane, between Grassy Plain and Bethel, lived Deacon Daniel Hickok, a very old deaf man, who for several years before his death sat in the pulpit in order to hear the services."

Upon his death, ownership of the family home on Blackman Avenue (it was then known as "the Old Lane"), would fall to Hickok's second son, Noah, as his oldest son had died in 1828. Noah would in turn pass the property on to his son-in-law, Abel Beers Blackman, a shoemaker who may have made use of Hickok's well-established shop and its materials. It is from Abel Beers Blackman that the street gains its name.

The house itself is one of only a handful of saltbox-style houses still left standing in Bethel. The exact date of construction is not known, but seeing as Daniel and Lucy Hickok were married in late 1769, the home may have been built at about that same time. The house has undoubtedly withstood the passage of nearly two and a half centuries, but its greatest mystery may always remain whether it truly played host to three distinguished guests on the night of the three generals.

3
Bethel's Tories

Those Who Chose Loyalty over Independence

When attempting to visualize New Englanders during the time of the American Revolution, the mind usually conjures up the image of a minuteman grabbing his musket and running off to do battle with the red-coated troops of the tyrannical King George III. Our region is proud to be known as "the birthplace of American independence," and subsequently little mention is made of those New Englanders who refused to support the move for American autonomy, those who valued loyalty more than independence. Bethel was home to some who shared this sentiment, but their story is one that has received scant attention in the many years since the end of American Revolution.

Now, to be sure, there were many individuals living within the area now designated as the town of Bethel who were ardent Patriots and sacrificed much in the cause of American liberty. There was Thaddeus Starr, who lived along Walnut Hill Road and served in the American army for three years, contracting smallpox and nearly losing his eyesight as a result.

There was another member of the Starr family, Captain Thomas Starr, an uncle to Thaddeus, who lived where the entrance to Willow Street exists today. He was one of the few citizens of our area to offer resistance to the British invasion force that attacked Danbury in April 1777. According to the *Starr Genealogy* of 1879, Thomas Starr "was struck down by a British officer with his cutlass, making a terrible wound across the head, taking the scalp and part of the face, and left for dead at the foot of Liberty Street. He was taken up by his friends and tenderly cared for, but never entirely recovered from the effects of the wound, and carried the frightful scar to his grave."

There was also Jesse Peck who lived along Sunset Hill Road and who entered the American army along with four of his sons. According to a Peck genealogy of 1868, "He and two sons, Nathaniel and Eliphalet, were taken prisoners and confined in New York in the prison ship 'Jersey' in the East River where they contracted smallpox, afterward were released and journeyed home on foot to Connecticut from which illness Jesse and his son, Nathaniel died."

A nineteen-year-old Bethel girl named Eunice Seeley also did her part. Seeley was the daughter of militia lieutenant James Seeley and lived on what is now Codfish Hill Road. She was in the process of returning home after visiting a friend in town, and upon viewing the approach of approximately eighteen hundred British troops on their way to capture military supplies in Danbury, young Eunice reportedly took action. Years later, her granddaughter remembered her relating the still vivid memory. "She described the gleam of the scarlet uniforms, and the flash of arms, and said that she dashed on toward Bethel, shouting, 'The British are coming! The British are coming!'"

Despite these accounts of heroism and self-sacrifice, the surviving records of the era also offer a glimpse of those who were just as willing to give their all in an effort to maintain their status as British royal subjects. In May 1778, the Connecticut Assembly, in an effort to both discourage and punish British loyalty among the state's inhabitants, passed "An Act for confiscating the Estates of Persons inimical to the Independence and Liberties of the United States within this State." As a result of this act, Bethel parishioners Benjamin Wilson, Hezekiah Benedict, Benajah Hoyt, Isaac Hoyt Jr., Samuel Hoyt, Hezekiah Benedict Jr., Benjamin Ferry and James Hoyt had their personal estates "declared forfeit by Fairfield County Court for the benefit of the state & their place of abode." Five of these individuals, along with one David Barnum, also had their real estate "ordered to be leased out for the use and benefit of the state." In addition, those considered to be the worst offenders—Hezekiah Benedict, Isaac Hoyt, Samuel Hoyt, Benjamin Ferry and Isaac Hoyt Jr.—had their real and personal estates officially confiscated. The Danbury probate records describe this last group as "having joined the enemies of the United States of America." The first three individuals on this list had all been among the seventy-one original members of the Second Ecclesiastical Society of Bethel founded on November 25, 1759. The remaining men (Isaac Hoyt Jr. and Benjamin Ferry) were the son of the aforementioned Isaac Hoyt and the son-in-law of Samuel Hoyt.

Some colonists may have indeed been staunch Tories who supported the British Crown for purely political purposes, but the members of this group had different motivations. In this instance, the men who had their properties confiscated were all followers of a Scottish minister named Robert Sandeman, who had arrived in Danbury in 1764 and died there in 1771. Sandeman's teachings and church practices were considered highly controversial at the time, but nonetheless he was able to establish churches in Danbury, Newtown and Bethel. (The Danbury Sandemanian Church was the last of its kind to exist in America and ceased to function in 1891.) The followers of the Reverend Robert Sandeman—or Sandemanians, as they were commonly called—advocated a return to the Christian church of the first apostles. Some of their practices included a rejection of formal ministers, preferring instead the election of their own church elders; a weekly Sunday dinner known as a love feast; and a kiss of brotherhood passed from member to member. At the outbreak of the Revolution, the Sandemanians found themselves in the midst of controversy after searching the Bible for spiritual guidance and deciding that it instructed them "to bind our consciences to be faithful and loyal subjects to our sovereign King George the Third, whom God preserve, to whose government we are heartily attached." They took as their guide Romans 13:1, which advises, "Let every soul be subject unto the higher powers. For there is no power but of God: the powers that be are ordained of God." With political fervor running high, these dissenters were viewed simply as traitors to the cause of American independence and were harshly treated as such.

What the local outcasts most greatly feared was possible violent retribution after the British destruction of Danbury in April 1777, and apparently for good reason. Four years after the war had ended, Sandemanian Samuel Hoyt, who lived at the foot of Hoyt's Hill on its eastern side (hence its name), petitioned the state to have his confiscated estate returned to him. In explaining why he had chosen to leave his home and go off with the British troops after their attack on Danbury, Hoyt recounted what had happened to a fellow Bethel Sandemanian, Hezekiah Benedict:

*That when the troops belonging to the King of Great Britain made an
excursion to Danbury in the year 1777 they passed by the dwelling house
of your petitioner, when your petitioner being at home, tarried at home till
he was informed and really believed that the justly incensed multitude of
the people threatened to put to death all those people who had remained at
their homes while the enemy was there, and that they had so far carried their
threats into execution as to fire upon one Hezekiah Benedict and his sons of
said Danbury and had shot one of Benedict's sons through the thigh, your
petitioner was therefore compelled through fear of his life to go off with said
enemy to Long Island.*

A passage in Bailey's *History of Danbury, Conn.*, published in 1896 seems
to speak of the same event but from the view of the attacker. It tells of
how Joseph Barnum of Danbury (now Bethel) had a son who was taken
prisoner by the British during the Danbury raid and subsequently died of
starvation in the notorious Sugar House Prison in New York City. Bailey's
History states, "His father, Colonel Joseph Barnum, was seriously affected by
the deplorable fate of his boy, and became so full of the spirit of vengeance,
that on the next day after getting the news he loaded his gun and started out
to avenge himself on sympathizers with the British. Seeing a Tory at work in
a field the half-crazed father fired at him, wounding him severely."

Samuel Hoyt's brother Isaac likewise had his property confiscated.
Records suggest that Isaac Hoyt's property was never restored to him and
that he immigrated to Nova Scotia, returning to the area only after the
war ended. His wife, Mary, however, seems to have been more successful.
Records from the Connecticut General Assembly of May 1777 provide the
following account:

*Mary Hoyt, the wife of Isaac Hoyt, then late of Danbury, showed to the
Assembly that she had ever been a good Whig and true friend to the rights
of her country, and that her husband, when the enemy entered Danbury,
being an enemy to his country, went off and joined the British, by which he
had justly forfeited his estate, both real and personal; and that the selectmen
had seized upon all the personal estate of her husband, by means of which
she was deprived of the necessaries of life, and asked the Assembly to order
that one-third part of the clear, movable estate should be given to her, and*

the use of one-third part of all the real estate, for her natural life, for her support. The Assembly ordered that said Mary Hoyt should have and enjoy one-third part of the personal and real estate during the pleasure of the Assembly.

Another story of note relating to Bethel loyalists of the Revolution is loosely described in an article written by Katherine LaValla in 1955 for a Bethel centennial booklet. In relating how some of the town's roads obtained their names, LaValla tells the legend of how Chimney Road in Stony Hill received its appellation:

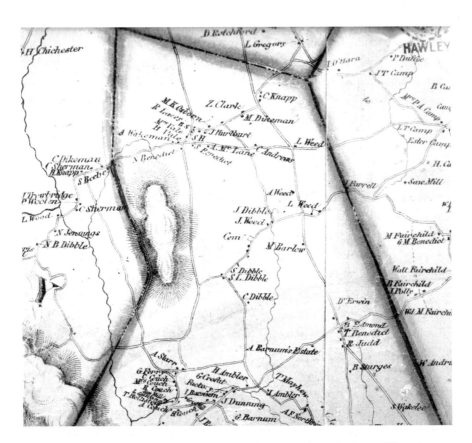

An 1858 version of *Clark's Map of Fairfield County, Connecticut,* shows the Stony Hill section of Bethel as it appeared at that time. Some of Stony Hill's Benedict family took a Loyalist stance in the American Revolution. As can be seen by this map, Stony Hill remained a relatively sparsely populated area for a very long time.

Chimney Road. An abandoned road running between Benedict Road and Payne Road in the Stony Hill district. The legend is that a family who were Tories had a large house there with an enormous chimney. During the Revolution, when local feelings were aroused, their house was burned with only the chimney remaining. However, the family hid in the chimney and escaped unharmed. For many years the tall chimney stood there and the road became known as Chimney Road. This story is disputed and I have been told that the house with the chimney was built by Capt. John Benedict, an ardent patriot. Still I hate to give up the original story, and as all records before the Revolution were burned when the British burned Danbury, there seems to be no way to prove or disprove it.

What LaValla did not know at the time of her article was that there could indeed be some slight historical plausibility to the legend. First, in stating that she had been told that the house in question had been built by Captain John Benedict and that he was an ardent Patriot, she was seemingly unaware of the fact that local militia member Captain Benedict had died in 1771, four years before the outbreak of hostilities between Britain and her American colonies. Benedict was survived by his wife, Ruth, and eight children, all of whom had already reached adulthood. His second oldest son, Josiah, according to "The Genealogy of Benedicts in America" was indeed a loyalist in the American Revolution. Records from the Connecticut General Assembly and of the town of Danbury clearly list Josiah Benedict among those Loyalists "whose personal estates were declared forfeit by the Fairfield County Court for the benefit of the state" in 1780. He may have even been an elder in the Sandemanian Church, as the meetinghouse itself was set off to his wife, Sarah, when his forfeited estate was dispersed. (The church was disparagingly referred to as "the kissing house" in the Danbury land records.)

At some later point, Benedict moved to New Brunswick, Canada, presumably because of his political loyalties, but eventually returned to the Danbury area and died there in April 1788. A more startling bit of evidence is the fact that Josiah Benedict's son Eli was one of two individuals who actually guided the British troops to Danbury from Fairfield at the time of the raid. Danburians learning of Eli Benedict's perceived treachery might certainly have seen the family home as a logical target for their anger.

Therefore, although the evidence to support this oral tradition is certainly circumstantial at best, it is safe to say that if this incident did occur, it was most likely an act of revenge that took place immediately following the British burning of nineteen homes, twenty-two stores and barns and a meetinghouse in Danbury's center on April 27, 1777.

Other Loyalists suffered similar fates to the ones described here, and the existing accounts of their experiences provide ample evidence that not all Bethelites desired "to dissolve the political bands" that had connected them with their mother country during America's epic war for Independence.

(*Note*: Prior to taking on the name Chimney Road the original stretch of dirt roadway that led up the steep rise from Payne Road to Benedict Road was referred to as "Jachin's Ridge." The "Jachin" of Jachin's Ridge was presumably Captain John Benedict's younger brother Jachin, who was born in 1727 and died in 1785. The current-day Chimney Road traces a small portion of the old abandoned road and provided the basis for naming the large 1960s housing subdivision Chimney Heights.)

4

The Reverend John Ely House

The house sits on a stately eminence overlooking Milwaukee Avenue. It is a distinguished structure with a distinguished past, and for well over two hundred years, it has been home to some of Bethel's most prominent citizens. Number 54 Milwaukee Avenue has a history that is strongly intertwined with that of our town, and an examination of the life of this one house renders an account of how our community has evolved over two-plus centuries. All available evidence points to the fact that this home was built for Bethel's second Congregational minister, the Reverend John Ely. The first deed indicating the purchase of land for the house possesses the date of March 19, 1792. On that day, Samuel Benedict and his wife, Phoebe, conveyed ten acres and 150 rods of land near Hoyts Hill to the Reverend John Ely, "reserving to ourselves the grain now growing on said piece of land with liberty to go on to said land and take said grain at the time of harvest." This deed is the earliest one to mention any purchase of property by Mr. Ely and also mentions that the land is bounded on the south by a highway, which would concur with the present location of the house.

As early as the autumn of 1791, the elders of the Congregational Church were looking for a home for their newly chosen minister. At a church meeting held on October 31 of that year, it was decided to "impower the societies [*sic*] committee to purchase a place for Mr. Ely and give their obligation for the same."

The Reverend John Ely House

The Reverend John Ely House, located at 54 Milwaukee Avenue, was built in 1792 for Bethel's second Congregational minister. The house was later home to Oliver Shepard, a hat manufacturer and state legislator who was instrumental in having Bethel incorporated as a town in 1855.

So it seems that the land may have been purchased, and the house built, with the assistance of funds provided by the new minister's grateful congregation. The Bethel parishioners were justified in being pleased with their new pastor, as he was a man of some accomplishment. Mr. Ely was born on June 14, 1763, the eldest child of Deacon Seth Ely and Lydia Reynolds Ely of North Lyme, Connecticut. The Reverend Ely was a member of the 1786 graduating class of Yale and was licensed to preach by the Middlesex Association of Ministers in 1788. He was called to preach in Bethel in September 1791 and, upon his acceptance, was ordained on November 30. For his efforts in leading his Bethel flock down the path of righteousness, Mr. Ely received an annual salary of sixty pounds plus forty loads of firewood.

A controversy arose in 1802 surrounding an anonymous letter that Mr. Ely had allegedly written to a friend by the name of Griswald. The communication contained disparaging remarks regarding some of Bethel's parishioners. After a committee of church members met with Mr. Ely to discuss the circumstances surrounding the explosive letter, the society voted on November 1, 1802, that it did "not wish to continue the Rev. John Ely as their minister any longer." Although this vote was later rescinded and a temporary reconciliation between minister and congregation was achieved, Mr. Ely and the church leaders agreed in January 1804 that it was best for him to leave, and he was formally dismissed on June 7, 1804. Mr. Ely would go on to serve other congregations in South Salem, New York, and North Madison, Connecticut. In 1827, he was making preparations to remove from Madison so that he might live with his son in central New York when he was thrown from his wagon. He held on for four days following the accident but died on November 9, 1827, at the age of sixty-five.

The next occupant of 54 Milwaukee Avenue was Mr. Ely's replacement as Bethel's Congregational minister, the Reverend Samuel Sturges, who purchased the home on April 9, 1806, the same day he was ordained in Bethel. Mr. Sturges and his wife, Betsey, would live in the house until his dismissal as minister in December 1811. The property passed into the hands of Eli Taylor, who lived just east on the opposite side of the road at what is now 51 Milwaukee Avenue.

In 1828, Mr. Taylor sold the property to Sherman Ferry, a hatter who constructed a hat shop on the premises. When Mr. Ferry sold the house and land to Dr. Ezra P. Bennett and his wife, Sarah, in 1836, the deed mentions a dwelling house, barn and "the privilege of the water conveyed on to said premises by means of leaden pipes by paying half of the expenses of repairs, reserving the hatter's shops thereon standing which are to be removed off within a reasonable time." The source of the water that was conveyed through the aforementioned pipes was a spring located in a field behind 51 Milwaukee Avenue, in what is now known as Andrews Park. The new owner, Dr. Ezra P. Bennett, was one of the area's most prominent physicians, and a short biography of his life can be found among the pages of James Bailey's *History of Danbury*, published in 1896. Dr. Bennett commenced his practice in Bethel in January 1828, but by the summer of 1837, only a year after purchasing the Milwaukee Avenue home, he was advertising the sale of the property in the *Danbury News*.

On August 17, 1837, the house and its grounds, now consisting of eight and a half acres, were sold to Oliver Shepard and his wife, Mercy. Prior to this, the Shepards had lived at what is now 125 Greenwood Avenue. Mr. Shepard was an illustrious figure in Bethel's history in that he was one of the town's leading hat manufacturers, a constable, a selectman, a justice of the peace and Bethel's first postmaster, serving from July 4, 1820, to July 25, 1825. Oliver Shepard was a state representative for Danbury in 1826 and served as state senator during the 1840s and 1850s. It was primarily through Mr. Shepard's efforts that Bethel was set off as a separate town from Danbury in 1855. In a way, Oliver Shepard might be regarded as the father of our town. Upon Mr. Shepard's death on February 22, 1861, the ownership of 54 Milwaukee Avenue, which was then called Liberty Street, passed to his wife, Mercy. After her death fourteen years later, the property was sold by their son William to Bradley Adams, who was employed at a local hat factory. Mr. Adams and his wife, Olive, would maintain ownership from 1876 until 1895. From 1895 until 1917, the home was owned by Bradley Adams's daughters, Sally A. Cole and Emily Adams.

The next owners, Robert and Jennie Keeler, would make the house their home from 1917 until 1920. Mrs. Keeler served as president of the Bethel Library's Ladies Auxiliary, as town librarian and as a member of the library's board of directors. There is a bronze plaque on display in the library that honors her many efforts. Other owners of the house have included: Stanley and Mary Wetmore from 1920 to 1923; Emma and Leonore Bruckner from 1923 to 1945; Kenneth and Lucille Mackenzie from 1945 to 1951; George and Ruth Bolz from 1951 to 1957; David and Margaret Higgins from 1957 to 1982; and Francy Searles from 1982 to 1987. The current owners, Jeffry and Maryan Muthersbaugh, purchased the home in 1987 and have since carried out a major restoration effort.

The home, which is on both the Connecticut and National Registers of Historic Places, still retains many of its original features, including the massive central stone chimney and its numerous fireplaces. The kitchen fireplace still retains its crane for hanging iron cooking utensils over an open fire, and there is a brick beehive oven to the right of the fireplace opening. There is a summer kitchen fireplace in the cellar that was used in the hottest months of the year when the coolness of the cellar made cooking over a roaring fire more tolerable. The attic still contains a smokehouse that was once used for curing meats, and most of the floors are original, as are many of the batten-style doors with their hand-forged iron latches. The front portico, the side sun porch and the kitchen addition in the rear of the home are the only features of the house that are of later vintage.

The grounds of the seven-room house possess several large maple trees and one colossal sycamore, which is probably as old as the house itself. The backyard contains a large barn that the Muthersbaughs have also restored and improved. Thus far, the couple has added a new kitchen wing in the rear of the house, replaced the roofs of both the house and barn with original-style wood shingles, repaired and strengthened the central chimney, fitted up the entire front with new clapboards, restored the sun porch on the house's east side, repainted the entire exterior of the house and made a multitude of other enhancements to both the home's charm and functionality. This being said, it is a fair guess that the Reverend John Ely House will continue to be a Bethel landmark for years to come.

5

Bethel's Historic Main Street Houses

B ethel's Main Street, although no longer the true center of our town, still contains many houses of historic importance. Here is a summary of their individual histories.

4 MAIN STREET: A Greek Revival- style house built about 1845 by Charles H. Shepard. The land on which the house was built belonged to Daniel Barnum from 1788 until his death in 1839. At that time, the property was transferred to Barnum's sons, Andrew and Daniel Jr. The two sons in turn sold the property in 1845 to Charles Henry Shepard, born in Bethel in October 1817. He died here on November 23,1895, aged seventy-eight years, one month, eighteen days. He was married in Brookfield on April 26, 1843, to Fanny Gregory, born in Brookfield November 6, 1818. She died in Bethel on January 12, 1899, at the age of eighty years, two months, six days. She was the daughter of Lewis and Hannah (Beebe) Gregory. The Shepards are buried in the Center Cemetery, their stones stating their dates of birth and death. Charles H. Shepard was a hatter in Bethel and represented the town in the Connecticut legislature in 1872. Charles and his brother Frederick owned a hat shop that stood on the site of what is now 40 Main Street, the home of the VFW and Bethel Historical Society.

6 MAIN STREET: An Italianate-style house built in 1871 for Samuel S. Ambler, a prosperous hat manufacturer who, along with his partner, George Munson Cole, owned and ran the Cole-Ambler hat factory that stood on the west side of Fountain Place (now known as P.T. Barnum Square). Ambler was also a Civil War veteran, having served in the Twentieth Connecticut Regiment, Company G, from September 2, 1862, until August 31, 1863. This house was patterned after the Harmon Taylor house, which stood on Greenwood Avenue where P.T. Barnum Plaza now stands. The Taylor home was demolished in 1965. Mention is made of the Ambler house being built in the December 20, 1871 issue of the *Danbury Times*. An article from a May 1873 issue of the *Danbury Times* later states, "S.S. Ambler is putting up a fine front fence. If the west end had condescended to have bowed its ribs a little, it would not felt quite so much above its neighbors." The carpentry work was done by the Gilbert Brothers (Eli, Philo and Henry), who operated a lumberyard and carpentry shop at the northeast corner of Elizabeth Street, near the old Bethel Railroad Station. The Gilbert brothers began business in 1858 and built many of the Victorian homes in downtown Bethel until about 1905, when they went out of the home building business.

10 MAIN STREET: A Greek Revival–style house built for Frederick Shepard around 1853. He was born in Bethel on May 8, 1815, and died here on January 3, 1894, at the age of seventy-eight years, seven months, twenty-six days. He was married in Bethel on November 10, 1839, to Eliza Hannah Smith. She was born in Bridgewater on April 20, 1817, and died in Bethel on August 5, 1896, at the age of seventy-nine years, three months, sixteen days. She was the daughter of Joseph and Martha (Wilmot) Smith. He was a hatter in Bethel and served terms as town clerk and judge of probate. He and his wife are buried in Center Cemetery. Their gravestones give the dates of birth and death.

Frederick Shepard and his brother Charles were the sons of Oliver Shepard (1783–1861), who lived at 125 Greenwood Avenue and later at 54 Milwaukee Avenue. Oliver Shepard was a hatter who came to Bethel from Newtown about 1806. The hat shop owned by Shepard stood at the northwest side of P.T. Barnum Square. Oliver Shepard apparently sold land to his son Charles, who in turn sold land to his brother Frederick for the purpose of building his home. Frederick Shepard, while serving as town clerk, had his office located on the southeast corner of his home lot. This office can be seen in a bird's-eye view of Bethel issued by O.K. Bailey and Company of Boston in 1879. The yard of the house today still shows a depression where the foundation of the office once stood. Frederick Shepard was responsible for enumerating the citizens of Bethel for the 1880 census.

16 MAIN STREET: A Federal-style home presumably built by Daniel Barnum (October 6, 1761–May 25, 1839) around 1790. Daniel Barnum was at first a joiner (carpenter) and cabinetmaker and so may have done the actual work of building the house. This Daniel Barnum was a first cousin to P.T. Barnum's father, Philo. The famous showman referred to him as "Uncle" Daniel Barnum. In 1825, Daniel Barnum sold this house to his daughter Anna and her husband, John Benedict III. The couple maintained ownership until 1844, when they moved to Wisconsin. The next owner was Dr. Hanford N. Bennett (1818–1868), who resided here from 1844 to 1853. At that time, the house was sold to another physician, Dr. Ransom Perry Lyon (1826–1863), who was an 1853 graduate of Yale University. During the Civil War, Ransom P. Lyon died of exposure and overwork while serving as the surgeon for the Twenty-eighth Regiment, Connecticut Volunteer Infantry, at the Siege of Port Hudson, Louisiana, on August 6, 1863.

Dr. Lyon's widow, Sophia, maintained possession of the property until 1871, when it was sold to the Danbury and Norwalk Railroad. During that year, a connecting stretch of railroad was built from Bethel to Hawleyville that allowed passengers and freight to be transferred from the Danbury and Norwalk line to the Shepaug Railroad line that ran north from Hawleyville to Litchfield. This Shepaug connecting link began at the Bethel station and then curved sharply to the east, passing through the area now occupied by the municipal center (built 1939), and ran across a forty-foot-long trestle over Wooster Street, where it then continued east along the north side of Main Street. The house now known as 16 Main Street originally sat at the base of Golden Hill Street. The house was moved eighty feet to the west in order to accommodate the tracks of the Shepaug connecting link. The hillside behind the house had to be blasted away, and even today the scars of drill bits and a broken drill bit itself can be found within the rocky cliff created by those railroad workers of long ago. The house next served as a boardinghouse for railroad workers until it was purchased by George M.

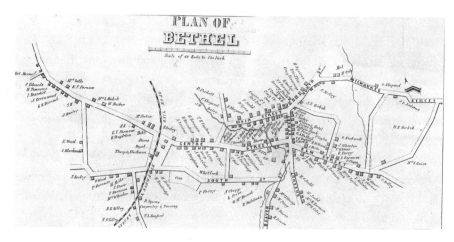

This view of Bethel's center dates from 1856, only one year after the town's official incorporation, and comes from *Clark's Map of Fairfield County, Connecticut*, created by Richard Clark of Philadelphia.

Cole in 1881. Cole is responsible for placing an addition on the structure's east end and creating a Victorian-style porch for its front.

GOLDEN HILL STREET: Golden Hill Street was cut through in the late summer of 1881 by George Munson Cole, who was then warden of the Town of Bethel. Cole had purchased the house at 16 Main Street in August 1881 and used property to the right of the house to create a road leading to Hickok Avenue at the top of the hill. Hickok Avenue had been cut through in December 1875.

23 MAIN STREET: This two-story Federal-style home was most likely built by Lemuel Beebe about the year 1819. It is in that year that Beebe purchased property from Nathan Seelye, who owned a hat factory to the east of where 23 Main Street now stands. Also to the west and south of this house once stood a tannery yard with a small dwelling house, a shop, bark house and tanning vats. The tannery seems to have been established by Jesse Curtis about the year 1806, when Curtis purchased property on this spot from Phineas Taylor. In 1816, Curtis sold his tan yard to Lemuel Beebe, who continued the business at least until 1858 as a map of that year identifies the site as being a place where saddles and harnesses were manufactured. The homestead on the property was purchased by adjoining landowner Nathan

Seelye in 1834, but it appears that Lemuel Beebe continued to live in the house for many years after that time. Nathan Seelye sold the homestead in 1865 to William Harrison Ferry, who is shown as living in this home on the 1867 *Beers' Atlas* map of Bethel.

27 MAIN STREET: This house is actually two houses in one. The left half of the structure seems to date back to well before the year 1800 and may have been the home of Zar Dibble, one of Bethel's earliest hatters. In 1802, Zar Dibble left Bethel for upstate New York and sold the house to a Timothy Taylor. The building was again sold in 1810 to two men named Lewis Gregory and Delceena Benjamin, who used the building as a hat shop. A year later, the building was sold to another hatter, Nathan Seelye, who continued to use the building for hatting purposes until 1816, when he sold the building and property to his son, Isaac Seelye (1793–1880). At about this time, the hatting business was moved elsewhere, and Isaac Seelye decided to build a fine new house for himself and adjoin it to the structure that had been converted to a hat shop. The house is an excellent example of Federal-style architecture, and the front entrance still maintains its fine window configuration and lead ornamentation. An identical front entrance can be found on page 118 of J. Frederick Kelly's 1924 work, *Early Domestic Architecture of Connecticut*. The eagle ornament found in the house's transom window is also shown on page 120 of Kelly's book. The illustrations are of the Cornwell House in Cheshire that is dated to circa 1820. That date would be in line with the 1816 construction date ascribed to this house. The small side street running north and south on the west side of the house still bears the name of Seeley Street as a testament to the family's role in Bethel's development.

31 MAIN STREET: (The following account was written before this house was destroyed by fire in February 2004. It is included to provide a historical record.) This house is an example of a late Federal style of architecture. The house was built just as the Federal style was being replaced by that of Greek Revival. The date of construction for this house can be fairly well pinpointed. The Danbury land records show that this plot of land was sold in 1813 by James Beebe and Timothy Taylor to Stiles Wakelee. At that time, there was no mention of a house on the property. The land was next sold by Stiles Wakelee in early 1816 to William M. Weatherill, and at this time

mention is made of a dwelling house. From this information, we can deduce that the house was built for Stiles Wakelee sometime between April 1813 and February 1816. The house was owned for a short period in 1817 by Phineas Taylor, grandfather of P.T. Barnum. Taylor in turn sold the house to Ammon Benedict, who sold the house in 1820 to Levi Beebe. Beebe is shown as still living here on the 1851 McCarthy map of Bethel, as well as maps from 1856, 1858 and 1867.

32 MAIN STREET: This house seems to have been built in the early 1830s by James H. Beebe. The first time the house is mentioned in the Danbury land records is in 1816, when it was sold by Beebe to Zera Benedict. Benedict owned a store and tailor shop farther east on Main Street on the opposite side of the road. Benedict once had in his employ a young seamstress by the name of Charity Hallett, who would later become the first Mrs. P.T. Barnum. Zera Benedict fell on hard times, and ownership of the house was returned to James H. Beebe. Benedict moved to Bristol, Wisconsin. In old land records, the property is said to be twenty rods (or 330 feet west of the Bethel Meetinghouse) with a dwelling house on said land. The house was sold in 1842 to Zadock Fairchild Judd. In 1871, while the house was still in Judd's possession, the Shepaug Railroad connecting link was put through, and its path took a course that followed the north side of Main Street. In order to accommodate the track, nearly all of the land in front of this house was removed, and a high stone retaining wall was constructed. The November 29, 1871 edition of the *Danbury News* mentions how the owner will be receiving financial compensation for losing a good deal of property. "Z.F. Judd will soon get quite a large amount as it cuts off all his front."

35 MAIN STREET: This house was most likely built about 1845 by Ezra P. Fairchild, who was a local merchant. Later, the house was purchased by the Congregational Church for use as a parsonage. The house had to be sold in 1867 in order to cover the cost of building the present church building.

43 MAIN STREET: This house seems to have been built as a store for William Kyle in 1871. The site of the house is in many ways more important than the house itself. A February 18, 1871 article in the *Danbury News* states:

A reminder of bygone days has been removed. The old building opposite I.H. Wilson's (4 Chestnut Street) which has stood so many changes, has just been torn down and W. Kyle is-erecting in its place a store which will be a branch of the one at the depot and will be just what is wanted up street, leaving out the beer and cider, and these left out, Kyle, we promise you a hearty support. The old building just removed has passed through more changes than any in town. Here it was that great P.T. Barnum made his first début as a businessman, first as a shop keeper, then as an editor (only think) under its roof the Herald of Freedom *first saw the light, which brought its author more darkness than light for a short time, but doubtless had much to do with shaping the future of this great man, who has become known and respected the world over, (we expect a free ticket to his new museum). The changes, it would not be well to follow as it would a tale unfold which would put Hamlet's ghost in the shade, but it has gone and let by-gones be by-gones.*

The corner yard of this home was also once the site of a house owned by Reuben J. Signor, who for many years was the ice man for much of Bethel in the days before modern refrigerators. (The ice pond that supplied his product can still be seen along the north side of the lower portion of Nashville Road Extension.) That same house was built by P.T. Barnum's grandfather Phineas Taylor in 1817. The home was badly damaged by fire on November 13, 1899, and torn down the following April.

6

Main Street's Second Meetinghouse and Congregational Church

They sit beside each other on Main Street, separated only by the old burying ground. One served as the Congregational Meetinghouse for only 22 years; the other has served as a home for Bethel's Congregationalists for 144 years—two churches built to serve the same parishioners within nearly two decades. If only boards, brick and stone could talk, what a tale this pair could tell. We know them today as the Second Meetinghouse and the Congregational Church of Bethel, and both are rich in history. In truth, these two churches are not the only buildings to have served Bethel's Congregationalists. Up until 1760, there was only one church of any kind that our forebears could attend, and that was the Congregational Meetinghouse on Main Street in Danbury. But by 1759, the portion of the flock residing in that part of Danbury that now encompasses Bethel was quite frustrated.

Their frustration was expressed to the colony's General Assembly in a petition that stated:

> *We your Hon. memorialists being (many of us) at least very remote from the publick worship of God where it is maintained and attended upon in the First Society and township of Danbury and so consequently cannot attend publick worship without grate cost and manefest inconvenience having large families etc. and the meeting house we now meet in being so full that it cannot accomidate the whole.*

So it was that the General Assembly granted permission for a second parish to be created for those citizens living in the southern part of Danbury. The petitioners had asked that their new society be named "Eastbury," but the Colonial Assembly thought that "Bethel," meaning "house of God" in Hebrew, was a better choice. The seventy-one members of this new society and their families lost no time in building their own meetinghouse. That first place of worship was occupied by May 1760 and measured forty-eight feet by thirty-six feet and twenty-one feet in height between joints and was covered with oak shingles three feet long. The building's interior remained unfinished until 1796, when a pulpit, gallery and pews were added. A steeple was constructed in 1818, and a bell was installed in 1828. Extensive repairs took place in 1832, and the old-style pews were replaced by slips.

This building served faithfully until July 21, 1842, when disaster struck. The *Danbury Times* of the following week provided this account:

> *On Wednesday night last, the ancient edifice occupied by the Congregationalists of Bethel as a place of worship, was entirely consumed by fire, together with a barn nearly adjoining belonging to Mr. David Lyon. The fire originated in the barn, and communicated from thence to the steeple of the meeting-house. Both buildings were reduced to ashes in about two hours from the time the fire was first discovered and although but three miles distant from this village, the circumstance was not known here until the following morning.*

Luckily, the church's record book, containing vital information dating back to 1759, was saved, and the event was later recorded in its pages by the church's clerk, Henry O. Judd. He wrote, "Meeting House destroyed by fire July 21st 1842" and surrounded his words with swirls of black ink. The loss of the church is made even more ironic by the fact that Bethel's first firehouse—or engine-house, as it was then called—stood in the front portion of the Congregational Cemetery and so was located directly next door.

The members of the church remained unflappable despite the conflagration, and in the following week's *Danbury Times*, they advertised the fact that they were prepared to receive proposals for building a meetinghouse in Bethel, fifty-two feet by thirty-eight feet. The job of building this new church was given to Rory Starr of Danbury for "the consideration of twenty-seven hundred and fifty dollars." Mr. Starr was a carpenter of considerable renown who operated a lumber mill on Elm Street in Danbury and was the first sawmill owner in the area to make use of the circular saw. He was so highly thought of that he represented Danbury in the General Assembly for three straight years in the early 1830s and was also in the state senate for one. He even served as a preacher in the Danbury Methodist Church. Starr had the new meetinghouse completed in time for a dedication ceremony on June 1, 1843.

The second church was built close to the site of the first but was situated exactly north and south, whereas the original church had faced east. The Second Meetinghouse would serve its congregation until May 11, 1865, when disaster would strike a second time. Just one month after the Confederate surrender at Appomattox and the assassination of President Lincoln, Bethel was the scene of a very peculiar meteorological phenomenon. The *Danbury Times* of May 18, 1865, described the event in the following manner:

A most destructive thunder-storm and whirlwind swept over this vicinity on Thursday evening. While in nearly every direction around us the damage sustained was more or less severe, we, occupying what may be called the centre, most signally, escaped the visitation. We note a few of the points where the storm struck the heaviest:

BETHEL—The force of the thunder gust, whirlwind, tornado, or whatever it was, seems to have been hurled against our unfortunate neighboring village of Bethel…the spire of the Congregational Church was struck and prostrated, breaking through the roof of the building, and lapping over on the siding at the rear. The bell fell to the first floor, and is supposed to be uninjured. The marble communion table was smashed. The organ fortunately escaped, and remains in position. It is feared that the building is damaged beyond successful repairing—the total amount of which is roughly estimated at $5,000.00. The sexton had lighted the Church for evening services just as the shower came up, but extinguished the lights and had barely crossed the street when the church was in ruins. A shudder follows the thought of how near the wreck came to being the tomb of the congregation.

Following this second catastrophe, the church leaders had to decide whether to repair the old house of worship or build an entirely new one. At a meeting on May 24, 1865, in the basement of the damaged church, it was decided to solicit donations to build a new church. The question regarding what to do with the remains of the old church now arose. The answer came on July 10, when it was determined "that the Society's [building] Committee be instructed to lease a portion of the old Burying Ground, next to the Engine-House, upon which to remove the Old Church, to be fitted up as a Hall; in the best manner they can, according to their judgment."

Just how the Second Meetinghouse made its way 165 feet west from its original location is not known, as the specifics of the event were not published in any of the newspapers of the time or in the records of the Congregational Church. It can be assumed that the relocation was made possible by using numerous jacks, rollers and teams of strong oxen, as this was the most common method used during the mid-nineteenth century. Moving buildings was quite common in the years before heavy traffic and numerous utility wires. Frugal New England Yankees rarely tore down buildings; any that were usable were more often "recycled."

The process may have involved first lifting the structure off of its foundation and then moving it directly forward into Main Street. At this point, the building may have been turned so that its entrance would now face east. Next, the building would have been moved backward in a westerly direction until it arrived just in front of where it was to eventually rest. Then it would have been directed a few yards north and jacked a full story into the air so that it might be placed atop a new foundation that would provide a level for stores facing onto the street. The only mention of the building's move appeared in the *Danbury Jeffersonian* of November 1, 1865: "The work on the new Congregational Church is progressing rapidly and favorably. The old church has been removed west of the cemetery, and is to be made into a Town Hall etc."

It appears that the original plan for the old church was for it to become a public hall that could be rented for social events such as meetings, dinners and dances. But since the town of Bethel had always used the basement of the Congregational Church for its town meetings since its inception in 1855, it seemed quite natural that the town would continue to use the only home it had ever known. And it appears from town records that public meetings were held in the old church building beginning in early 1866. By this time the building had acquired the name Judd's Hall, owing to the fact that it had been purchased by William A. Judd, who lived directly across the street and who was a deacon in the Congregational Church at just the time they were interested in having their old place of worship removed. Judd apparently purchased the building and moved it to a piece of property he had acquired in 1860 that was then occupied by a hat factory run by two brothers, Frederick and Charles Shepard. William A. Judd finished off the store space on the first floor of his new hall, which would eventually house at least two to three stores, the town clerk's office, the post office and the town jail. Unfortunately, Judd was also employed as the cashier of the First National Bank of Bethel and when the bank failed in 1868; his lost investments caused him to declare bankruptcy. Judd's Hall was then purchased by Nehemiah B. Corning, who in turn sold it to the Town of Bethel in November 1868 for just less than $4,000.

Over time, the building would go through many changes. It seems that a one-story addition was created on the west side of the building in 1876 to provide additional store space. Bigger changes came in 1880, when the local National Guard unit officially referred to as Company A, 8th Regiment, eyed the building as a new home. They had formerly met at Fisher's Hall, now known to us as the old Opera House. They agreed to rent the hall as an armory providing the town made certain changes to the building. The *Danbury News-Times* of March 31, 1880, described the unit's requirements: "In the first place the band room is to be raised to the height of the hall…(The band room mentioned was the 1876 addition on the building's west side.) This is to be divided in two rooms, one to be used as a reception room, the other to contain the company's arms and equipment. Then… that the galleries to be taken out and a floor put in making two stories of the present hall the upper one to be used for a drill room." The town agreed to Company A's requests as long as the cost was not to exceed $1,000. The Gilbert Brothers, local builders who had their place of business on Elizabeth Street, completed the alterations by May 1880, and the National Guard unit immediately took occupancy.

The town continued to use the building for public meetings on a regular basis until 1939, when town meetings were moved to the new high school, now the Bethel Municipal Center. The building languished somewhat over the next several years, only being used occasionally by the Bethel Drum Corps and Bethel Grange. The town offices by this time had been moved to 116 Greenwood Avenue across from P.T. Barnum Square.

In 1947, the Town of Bethel sold the then 104-year-old edifice to the Veterans of Foreign Wars to be used as a meeting place for local post No. 935. The post immediately began a fundraising drive to make improvements in the hall, and through its efforts the first floor of the building was modernized, the exterior was re-sided and new windows were installed on the building's street side. The post's building fund drive, however, did not permit a restoration to be made to the building's upper floor. A fire there in the 1920s had done considerable damage. In 1985, the Bethel VFW and the Bethel Historical Society entered into an agreement wherein both groups would share ownership of the Second Meetinghouse. In 1987, an effort was begun by the co-owners of the building formally known as the Veteran's Holding Corporation to restore the exterior of the building and to renovate the interior so that it might be utilized as a town museum, meeting hall and research library. The restoration of the

A 1956 postcard view of the Veterans of Foreign Wars Hall at 40 Main Street. The building was originally built in 1843 and served as the second meetinghouse for Bethel's Congregationalists. It was damaged by a small tornado in 1865 and moved from its original site, repaired and refitted as the town hall. Today, it is jointly owned by the VFW and the Bethel Historical Society.

building's exterior was achieved, and a later phase included the renovation of the second and third floors of the 1876 addition. The building still awaits the renovation of the main area of the second floor, which had originally been utilized for church services. Presently this space serves as a storage area for the historical society.

Immediately following the removal of the 1843 house of worship, work was begun for the building of a new one. Beginning with a sixty-dollar contribution from the West Street Congregational Society of Danbury, the Bethel parishioners set to work collecting the needed funds. After having their first church burn to the ground and their second one destroyed by a tornado, it seems the Congregationalists took a cue from the story of "The Three Little Pigs" and this time decided to build with brick. Church fairs and festivals were held and speakers gave appearances, with all of the resulting proceeds going to the church building project. Among the luminaries who lent their oratory skills in support of the effort were the honorable Orris S. Ferry, the only Bethel native to ever serve in both the U.S. House of Representatives and the U.S. Senate, and none other than P.T. Barnum, who gave his well-known lecture on "The Art of Money-Getting."

The effort to complete the new church was going well with a few exceptions. One such exception is evidenced in an article appearing in the Danbury paper of November 29, 1865: "Yesterday morning the scaffolding on the new church gave way and fell to the ground, a distance of some 60 feet, and with it a man who was carrying brick. He was taken up and carried home, and it is feared he will not recover. We did not learn the man's name. Two other men who were on the scaffolding escaped injury." Ensuing issues of the paper gave no indication of the unfortunate workman's fate.

Along with this accident, the building effort met great difficulty raising enough money to complete the elaborate church design it had selected. The parish was even forced to sell its parsonage at 35 Main Street to help cover the cost of the new church. Some were not even sure they liked the plan of the progressing structure. A Danbury reporter noted, "One corner does encroach upon the old cemetery. Another almost protrudes into a brick dwelling and livery stables, another corner is decidedly in the street, and the remaining one must be somewhere else or nowhere." All hardships and criticisms were overcome by January 1867, and on the twenty-third of that

A 1911 postcard view of the Congregational church at 46 Main Street. The building was completed in 1867 and was built in the Italianate Revival style of architecture. The brick structure located immediately to the right of the church was demolished in 1959 to make way for a parish hall. The house shown farthest to the right still survives but now has an entrance that faces Maple Avenue rather than Main Street.

month the structure was dedicated by the Reverend F.J. Jackson of Danbury and the local paper now spoke of the church in glowing terms: "The church shows excellent design and workmanship being one of the neatest churches, internally, in this part of the country." The church was indeed unique, incorporating a slate roof with colored design and two towers, one housing a bell and the other a clock, the latter of which was originally topped with a weather vane.

The church would fare much better than its two predecessors, although a fire on March 17, 1926, did badly damage the church's interior, destroying the pulpit and choir loft and causing the loss of the church organ. Yet the church members decided not to abandon their longstanding home and voted instead to make repairs. The church was rededicated on January 2, 1927. In 1934, a side entrance was added near the east front of the building. In 1959, a brick dwelling house dating back to 1851 on the right side of the church was razed to make way for a new parish house that was completed in January 1960. In 1993, a major renovation of the church took place that included exterior paint, a new roof and gutters and a

Bethel's Congregational Church at 46 Main Street as it appeared during Sunday services in 1956. A lack of parking space has always been a problem for the church that has occupied the same piece of ground since 1760.

newly designed front entrance. Most recently, in 2009, the church joyfully celebrated its 250th year of existence.

The Second Meetinghouse and the Congregational Church are two buildings that have certainly served Bethel well over the years—and show promise to serve for many more.

7

Greenwood Avenue

The Heart of Bethel

M ost Bethelites travel Greenwood Avenue almost every day of their lives. But how many of us have stopped to wonder how our town's main thoroughfare got its name or why our Main Street is not our main street? For those who are curious, here are the answers.

The road we now call Greenwood Avenue is part of probably the oldest road through the center of Bethel, although the original path of the road was much different from today. A traveler of the 1700s on a journey from Fairfield to Danbury would have passed from Redding to Bethel along Sunset Hill Road, on to Putnam Park Road and then over Hoyt's Hill. At the bottom of the western side of the hill, the traveler would arrive at the first portion of today's Greenwood Avenue. (The portion of Greenwood Avenue that runs from the bottom of Hoyt's Hill to Milwaukee Avenue was not cut through until 1845.) Once on Greenwood Avenue, the visitor to Bethel would pass west along the road until he met what is now Chestnut Street. Here the traveler would have to turn right on Chestnut and then left on Main Street. (The portion of Greenwood Avenue lying between Chestnut Street and P.T. Barnum Square was not put through until the early 1830s.) From Main Street, one would turn left on the portion of Wooster Street where P.T. Barnum Square is now located. Then, at P.T. Barnum Square, one would turn right on today's main thoroughfare once more, until reaching a point directly in front of the library. Here, the roadway curved to the left and passed through

The intersection of Greenwood Avenue and Depot Place as it appeared in the early 1950s. *Courtesy of the Danbury Museum & Historical Society.*

A view looking west along Greenwood Avenue near P.T. Barnum Square from a postcard postmarked in 1933.

where the old railroad station now stands. The trip through Bethel would then continue west along South Street until reaching Blackman Avenue. Here the journey would venture right on Blackman Avenue and then, at the avenue's end, turn left back on Greenwood Avenue. The area in between the library and St. Mary Church was apparently mostly marshland for a long while, so the earliest course of the road sought to avoid this trouble spot.

At some point in the first half of the nineteenth century, the marshland was filled and a more direct route was created that avoided the area of Depot Place, South Street and Blackman Avenue. During the 1880s, a horse-drawn trolley system was installed that would carry passengers from downtown Danbury to today's P.T. Barnum Square. The horses pulling the trolley found it too difficult to traverse the incline of lower Main Street, so what had been up to that time "the heart of town" was now somewhat shunned. When an electric trolley was installed in 1895, the tracks were extended along Greenwood Avenue to its intersection with Milwaukee Avenue. When the railroad tracks of the Shepaug Railroad's connecting link to Hawleyville were installed on the north side of Main Street in 1871, most merchants decided to move their businesses to Greenwood Avenue, seeing it as a safer and more profitable location.

Greenwood Avenue, Bethel, Conn.

Greenwood Avenue as it appeared in 1906. The house shown farthest to the right was located on the site of the present entrance to the Dolan Shopping Plaza. A trolley car can be seen in the distance.

Bethel's well-traveled esplanade derives its name from John Greenwood Jr., who was born in Cambridge, England, in 1817. His father, John Greenwood Sr., brought his family to America and became the fifth minister of Bethel's Congregational Church, serving from 1838 to 1842. During his early years, the younger Greenwood worked in the hatting trade under the employ of Captain Isaac H. Seeley in a hat shop that stood on the present site of the Phineas Park Apartments. About the year 1848, Greenwood traveled to New York to find work with another Bethelite: P.T. Barnum. For the next twenty years, Greenwood would serve as assistant manager of Barnum's museums, his confidential agent and treasurer. Barnum once

John Greenwood Jr. (1817–1876), who served as P.T. Barnum's assistant manager at his American Museum in New York City. He was later appointed to the position of U.S. consul to Brunswick, Germany, by President Ulysses S. Grant and is the individual for whom Greenwood Avenue is named.

described him as being "honest to a penny." Greenwood was sent to the Middle East twice during the 1860s on museum business. According to Barnum biographer Arthur H. Saxon, Greenwood was part of the Quaker City expedition described in Mark Twain's novel *Innocents Abroad*. Upon his return home from his first trip, Greenwood enthralled his fellow Bethelites with a magic lantern show on the wonders of the holy land in the then recently completed Fisher's Hall (today's Opera House). In 1873, Greenwood was chosen by President Ulysses S. Grant to serve as U.S. consul to Brunswick, Germany. He was serving in that capacity when he died on February 9, 1876. The cause of death was recorded as being a carbuncle, a painful inflammation of the skin and underlying tissue. (In August 1868, Greenwood had undergone having his right arm amputated below the elbow due to the effects of an earlier carbuncle on his hand.) His remains were returned to the United States, and he lies buried in Bethel's Center Cemetery on South Street with a headstone that reads: "For fidelity to duty, for strict and undeviating integrity and other rare qualities of mind and heart loved and mourned by not a few."

Naming the road for Greenwood was not truly done as a tribute; rather, it was so named owing to the fact that it passed by his home and by a large portion of land owned by his family on the site of what is now Dolan Plaza. Greenwood lived in a house that still stands nearly opposite the south entrance to Farnam Hill Road. Greenwood had married Catherine Farnam in June 1841. Her father, Ethel T. Farnam, who lived in the large white house on the corner of Greenwood Avenue and Farnam Road, is the individual for whom Farnam Road is named. Greenwood may have played a role in having the area between Blackman Avenue and Depot Place opened as an improved roadway. Originally, the name, Greenwood Avenue was only applied to the area from Beach Street east to the railroad crossing. The portion of the road

This 1909 postcard shows what was then known as Elm Street and is now known as upper Greenwood Avenue. An electric trolley car run by the Danbury and Bethel Street Railway Company, which operated from 1895 until 1926, is seen in the distance.

The Sycamore Drive–In Restaurant at 282 Greenwood Avenue as it appeared in the early 1950s. The restaurant first opened in 1948 and has been an enormously popular eatery ever since. *Courtesy of the Danbury Museum & Historical Society.*

This view of the intersection of Greenwood and Dimond Avenues comes from a postcard dating from 1915. The hillside shown at the left would later be excavated to make way for a service station, commercial stores and the Sycamore Drive-In Restaurant. The buildings shown in the distance were replaced by a shopping center in 1957. The original spelling was "Dimond" Avenue, not "Diamond," as it stems from a Bethelite's last name rather than the gemstone.

Greenwood Avenue

A postcard from 1909 showing East Street, or today's upper portion of Greenwood Avenue, near its intersection with Hoyt's Hill Road. The house shown at left had only been recently built in 1905.

A postcard from 1956 that shows Greenwood Avenue looking east, as seen from the front lawn of the Bethel Methodist Church.

Greenwood Avenue on a summer's day in the early 1950s is shown in this photo taken from the vantage point of the Methodist church driveway at 143 Greenwood Avenue.

northwest of Beach Street was commonly referred to as Benedict's Corner until about the turn of the century. The portion of the road we today call Greenwood Avenue, running from the railroad tracks east to Chestnut Street, was known as Center Street. From Chestnut Street east to the bottom of Hoyts Hill was known as Elm Street, and the portion running from the bottom of Hoyt's Hill to the intersection of Milwaukee Avenue was known as East Street. On October 18, 1934, a special town meeting was held where it was decided to merge Center, Elm and East Streets with Greenwood Avenue. Since this new extended road would require renumbering all of the properties along its route, the idea of renaming the road was also discussed. Main Street and Barnum Avenue were the two suggestions put forth, but in the end, Greenwood Avenue was chosen without any protest. Now, over seventy-five years later, the roadway continues as Bethel's main artery and as the one street that most distinguishes our town.

8

Old Roads
and Turnpikes

Whoever said, "The shortest route between two points is a straight line" wasn't around when Bethel's roads were being laid out. New England's topography has always been a challenge to road builders, and our town's terrain was certainly no exception. Many of the winding roads Bethelites traverse today are centuries old and have been used by generations of our predecessors, with many of them following their ancient, original courses. With the help of several historic sources, the history surrounding some of these venerable byways can be rediscovered.

One of the earliest references to roads still in use today can be found in the petition that helped set Bethel off as a second parish of Danbury. The boundaries of the new parish would be defined by several natural features but would also include "the highway on the east of [East] swamp and by said highway to the highway called woodbury old road." The first highway mentioned in this 1759 document describes what we today call Payne Road. Payne Road obtained its name from Hugh Payne, who had a home on the east, or Bethel, side of the road in the early half of the twentieth century. Like many other roads in town, this road has lost its apostrophe *s* and was initially known as Payne's Road. Many drivers who curse the narrowness of Payne Road, which still divides Bethel from Danbury, would probably find little solace in knowing that they drive a road that was already well worn over 250 years ago. The second road referred to as the "Woodbury old road" has evolved into Route 6.

This postcard image dates from about 1915 and shows an early automobile presumably traveling along what would become known as Dodgingtown Road or Connecticut Route 302.

Descriptions of Bethel's earliest roads can also be found in the yellowed land records of Danbury's city hall. When British troops burned Danbury in 1777, all of the town's land records were destroyed. This included descriptions of all of Danbury's roads.

In January 1778, the Connecticut General Assembly instructed the town to produce a survey of all of its roads and to enter a description of each into the new land records. This survey still exists, and within its pages one can find mention of many roads that are today located within the boundaries of Bethel.

For example, road number 90 of the survey is described as "a highway from Fairfield Road to Norwalk Road across the hill near Deacon Stephen Trowbridge's house, said highway to be two rods wide." The road described is now known as Griswold Street. The Fairfield Road is today known as Greenwood Avenue (Route 302) and the Norwalk Road is Grassy Plain Street (Route 53). Deacon Stephen Trowbridge's house still stands at 63 Grassy Plain Street (the width of the road—two rods—would equal thirty-three feet, as one rod equals sixteen and a half feet.)

Road number 100 of the survey is presented as "one highway beginning at Bethel Meeting House running to the Sawmill Brook near Capt. Joseph

Old Roads and Turnpikes

Abandoned Bridge, Bethel, Conn.

A 1907 postcard presents a view of an abandoned bridge in Bethel. Although the exact location is not known, one can clearly see that the bridge was not truly abandoned judging by the tracks left in the dirt road. During the twenty years following the date of this image, many local roads would undergo major improvements owing to the increasing popularity of automobiles.

Starr four rods wide and from thence across walnut tree hill to the cross road two rods wide." This entry describes today's Maple Avenue and Walnut Hill Road, running from the Congregational church up to the point where Walnut Hill Road meets Turnpike Road at the end of a very steep incline. On the subject of turnpike roads, Bethel was located along several of them. A book entitled *The Turnpikes of New England*, published in 1919 and written by Frederic J. Wood, contains a great deal of information concerning turnpikes of our area. The Norwalk and Danbury Turnpike was created by an act of the Connecticut General Assembly in October 1795 and was to extend from Semi Pog (Sympaug) Brook in Danbury (now Bethel) to Belden's Bridge in Norwalk. This is essentially the same path the road follows today under the name of Route 53. Sympaug Brook passes beneath Route 53 at just about the same point where Grassy Plain Street becomes Turkey Plain Road and Route 53 ends in Norwalk at the Norwalk River, not far from Belden Avenue.

A turnpike company calling itself the Fairfield, Weston and Reading Turnpike Company was set up in 1797 to improve the road from the meetinghouse in Bethel to a point in Weston. This road would have been made up of what are today Nashville, Turkey Plain, Redding and Georgetown Roads. What is now Plumtrees Road was once part of "The Middle Turnpike," begun in 1803, which extended from Hartford to Danbury and passed through Farmington, Bristol, Plymouth, Watertown, Woodbury, Southbury, Newtown, Bethel and on into the center of Danbury. The road, which was commonly known as the Hartford and Danbury Turnpike, or sometimes by local people as the Newtown Turnpike, would have come to Bethel from the flagpole in Newtown via Castle Hill Road, Great Hill Road, Plumtrees Road and then on to Taylor Road, Walnut Hill Road, Turnpike Road, Shelter Rock Road and up over Shelter Rock Road into Danbury. The Fairfield County Turnpike, which was begun in 1834, had its start at the north end of the Black Rock and Weston Turnpike and continued on through Weston, Easton and Newtown into Bethel and finally terminating at "the four corners" in Brookfield. The road's path would have taken travelers along Westport Road in Easton, on to Stepney Road and

A 1910 postcard that shows a hay wagon passing the point where Maple Avenue and Maple Avenue Extension diverge. The structure in the distance was located near the entrance of today's Plumtrees Heights condominium complex. The large sycamore tree shown at the right survived until about the year 2000.

Hattertown Road in Monroe and on into Newtown. In Newtown, the turnpike followed Dodgingtown Road to Shelley Road on the Newtown and Bethel border. It then traveled along the now-abandoned portion of Shelley Road to Old Hawleyville Road, then on to Stony Hill Road in Brookfield and finally along Junction Road to Federal Road (Old Route 7).

But probably the most fascinating old turnpike to wind its way through Bethel was the ill-fated Sherman and Redding Turnpike that was begun in 1834. The road began at a point on the Newtown Turnpike just west of the present Greenbush Road in Redding. It then traveled north to Lonetown Road, then east onto Putnam Park Road. Next it traveled north along today's Route 58 until it reached a point just south of Hoyt's Hill Road. Here the road traveled along a now-abandoned easterly route until it met Route 302. It then crossed Route 302 and continued along a path near the Bethel Middle School and came out on Plumtrees Road. The turnpike then crossed over Plumtrees and continued on until meeting Taylor Road. From Taylor, the path led on Walnut Hill Road, Shelter Rock Road and a short stretch of Payne Road. The turnpike then diverged from Payne, taking a lower, more westerly route. It then reemerged at Route 6 where the entrance road to the Scholastic Publishing Co. is now located. The road crossed over the path of today's Route 6 and Interstate 84 and onto the course of the present Mountain View and Sunrise Roads, continuing north until reaching the current intersection of Federal and Candlewood Lake Roads. From this point, the turnpike followed a route that was parallel, but just west of, the current Candlewood Lake Road. The road then took a course that would today be located beneath the waters of Lake Candlewood, disappearing at Sunset Cove Road and reappearing near Candlewood Isles Road and its intersection with Route 39. The turnpike then continued on the present path of Route 39 into the center of Sherman.

According to *Wood's Turnpikes of New England*, "A petition filed in 1846 declared that the turnpike was never demanded by public necessity or convenience and for six years it had been 'wholly and entirely abandoned,' and consequently was impassable and useless." A local historian of the 1920s, Henry B. Belts of Danbury stated in a monograph written in 1921 that

> *this turnpike Co. received a charter from the state legislature in 1834 and the Co. was practically bankrupt before it was finished. The land purchased*

A 1909 view of a stone bridge located along Route 302 in the Elmwood section of Bethel near the present day St. Mary Roman Catholic Church. Not long after this photo was taken, the road was straightened for improved automobile traffic. A new bridge was constructed, and the old bridge is now part of a driveway to a private residence.

between the Danbury and Newtown Highway (Route 6) and the Danbury and Brookfield Highway (Federal Rd.) was never paid for nor deeds given and the contractor for this section never received his pay and the owners kept their land and closed up this section between 1840 and 1850—part of the other sections are used for town roads.

Reminders of the old Sherman–Redding Turnpike still remain to this day. In Bethel, we have Turnpike Road, probably so named because it led from Walnut Hill Road down a steep hill to the Sherman Turnpike Road. (It may also have acquired this name from having been a small portion of the Middle Turnpike of 1803.) This road was truncated sometime within the last sixty years and exists now as a dead end road. Redding still has a Sherman Turnpike Road. Danbury has its Old Sherman Turnpike Road, and Brookfield has roads called Old Sherman Turnpike and Old Turnpike Road. Betts also stated in his 1921 work that there was a toll gate in Brookfield near the White Turkey Inn. This spot is today occupied by the Candlewood Plaza shopping center at the northwest corner of Federal and Candlewood Lake Roads. According to Betts, the tolls collected were not enough to pay

Maple Avenue is shown in a postcard dating from 1912. Milwaukee Avenue can be seen branching off from Maple Avenue at the right. This road then took a sharp right turn before heading down toward an area known as "The Glen." Much later, the lower part of Milwaukee Avenue was truncated to allow for the creation of a four-way intersection that would provide greater traffic safety.

the keeper. It seems the turnpike was apparently ill timed, as the Housatonic Railroad was completed in 1840, and from that point on much of the freight that traveled north through this area went by rail rather than by horse-drawn wagon. Bethel's roads seem to have a history that suits them—long, winding and unpredictable but still pleasant to travel down.

9

The Early Days of the Bethel
Railroad Station

For well over a century, the old Bethel railroad station in Depot Place has been a fixture of our community. The railroad first came to Bethel in 1852. In March of that year, service began between Danbury and Norwalk with one round trip daily at a speed of eighteen miles an hour. Bethel was a ten-minute trip from the end of the line in Danbury and, at first, probably had very few townspeople riding the train for any reason other than curiosity.

The first official train station building seems to have been completed in 1852 or early 1853. A train station is shown on an 1851 map of Bethel on the west side of the track opposite the old depot location, but it was probably only the first proposed site since the railroad was not yet in operation. A succeeding 1856 map shows the old station in its present location. The original structure served the community's needs until December 15, 1898, when it was consumed in a mysterious conflagration. A rediscovered news article from the *Danbury News* of December 21, 1898, tells the story:

> The Bethel depot was completely destroyed by fire Thursday morning at about 12:30 o'clock. The fire was first discovered by a man named Durkin, who was attending the gates at the Greenwood Avenue crossing. Mr. Durkin went to the station to fix the fires, when he discovered the flames breaking through the ceiling just over the telegraph table in the ticket office. He immediately gave the alarm, and the members of the fire companies

were notified shortly after by the blowing of the whistle at Edwin Short's [hat] factory.

When the firemen reached the scene, the flames had gained such headway that the building was beyond saving. It was a hot fire and the firemen worked hard to get it under control. The flames were finally extinguished, leaving only a small portion of the framework, and here and there a part of the siding. There was some freight in the part of the depot used for that purpose, but it was all saved, being taken out by those first to reach the burning building. The employees about the station say they have no idea how the fire originated. It might have been caused by a spark from a locomotive which set fire to the roof, burning through the garret, where it must have been burning for some time before being discovered.

Temporary quarters in which to transact railroad business will be furnished by the company, to be used until a new depot can be built. The building was one of the oldest on the Danbury division, having been erected some time in 1853. Improvements had been made from time to time, as more room was required. Bethel will probably get a good sized station when the new one is erected, which is needed on account of the summer traffic up the Shepaug road, which has greatly increased a few years past. "All of the express trains from New York bring many city people for Litchfield and other points up the Shepaug during the summer season."

The work of building the new station was most likely slowed by winter weather and was not completed until the following spring. The *Danbury News* of May 10, 1899, stated, "The platform is being built about the new station and the rubbish cleared up around the premises. The depot will soon be ready to occupy." An article appearing in the May 24 issue of the same paper reads:

The interior of the new station is fitted up very comfortably. The waiting room is neatly finished off and furnished with all of the accommodations necessary. The ticket and telegraph office is in the center of the building, between the freight and passenger departments. Agent McMahon has a cosy [sic] little office, and just opposite is a small baggage room, which will be in charge of Baggagemaster Beaupain. The new station, although not a large one, will probably meet all requirements, and is certainly substantially built and nicely arranged.

A 1912 postcard view of the Bethel Depot. The structure was built in 1899, replacing an earlier building that was constructed in 1852 and burned down in 1898.

Ten years after its construction, remodeling was already taking place at the station, as evidenced in this August 10, 1909 article from the *Danbury News*:

That the improvements in and about the Bethel railroad station are soon to be begun is indicated by the arrival of considerable material. Lumber has been sent and is now stored in the freight house for remodeling the station itself. The waiting room is to be considerably enlarged by adding to the present room, the present freight business office and a large part of the room now utilized for freight on the south of the offices. A portion of the south end of the building is to be reserved for a baggage room. Several coal bins have been removed north of the Bethel feed elevator, where the new freight depot is to be built, and it is expected that this will be occupied before the depot is remodeled. Already ties for building the new freight tracks have been received.

Another splendid improvement which is to be made is the placing of crushed stone about the station, a carload of stone having reached here for that purpose. A coating of similar material was placed on the roadway a year or two ago with good result, but this has been ground to dust, and a new coating was badly needed.

The Early Days of the Bethel Railroad Station

An additional change to the station that helped provide its own unique appearance was the extension of the platform, which is described in a March 1910 issue of the *Danbury News*:

> *The long platform on the west side of the railroad passenger station is to be extended about one hundred feet on the north end, running out nearly or quite to the Greenwood Avenue crossing. This improvement is being made so that passengers may be landed on the platform, instead of on the ground, as it has often been necessary to do when there was a long train. In order to transfer baggage, the baggage cars must halt where it is most convenient for making a quick transfer, and often when this is done, passengers are obliged to leave or board the train at some distance beyond the platform. This is inconvenient for everyone, but especially so for aged or infirm persons, as it makes a much higher step than from the platform. The work of tearing up the ground was commenced this morning. It is said that the work of building the new freight depot in the freight yard, which has long been promised, is to be commenced in the near future.*

Coal-powered steam locomotives gave way to electric ones and then to diesel. The station continued to be utilized for commuter traffic until 1996,

The Terry Lumber Company on the southeast corner of Elizabeth Street and Front Street and the old Bethel railroad depot as they appeared in the late 1940s. *Courtesy of the Danbury Museum & Historical Society.*

The old Bethel depot as seen from the intersection of South Street and Depot Place as it appeared in the early 1950s. *Courtesy of the Danbury Museum & Historical Society.*

when it was replaced by a newer facility farther along the line situated on the west side of Durant Avenue. This was done primarily to alleviate the traffic snarls that resulted along both Greenwood Avenue and South Street when commuter trains stopped to board and discharge passengers, and for a long time the lack of adequate parking posed an additional problem. After the creation of the new station, the old one initially found new life as an art studio and received extensive repairs in 2003. Later, in 2011, the depot obtained an even greater renovation when it was occupied by the Bethel Cycle Shop.

10

Bethel's Commerce and Industry in the 1790s

The Bethel of the 1790s was quite an active spot with a great deal of industry and commerce taking place. Approximately 220 years ago, Bethel was still part of Danbury and would remain so until 1855. It had, however, been set off as a separate parish and had been referred to as "the Second Ecclesiastical Society" of Danbury's Congregational Church since 1759. When the first national census was taken in 1790, it was found that Danbury had achieved a population of 3,029 citizens, and 779 of those individuals were officially categorized as "free white males, over sixteen years and upward." Seven hundred and four more were listed as being "free white males, under sixteen years." The number of "free white females" was calculated to be 1,503. Those who fell into the category of "all other persons" were listed at amounting to twenty individuals, and Danbury's slave population was put at twenty-three.

No separate figures were provided for the parish of Bethel, but by comparing those individuals listed in the 1790 census with contemporary land records, it can be fairly estimated that the number of citizens living in the part of Danbury that later became Bethel would have amounted to 790 people. Bethel possessed roughly 170 families with the average family being made up of 5.04 persons per household, just under the national average of 5.06. (By the time Bethel was set off as a separate town in 1855, the proponents of the separation claimed Bethel had achieved a population of over 2,000. When the next census was taken in 1860, it was revealed that our actual number of residents was 1,711.) Of the 790 individuals calling Bethel their home, 5 were slaves. Two of these individuals were owned by Josiah Starr, who lived at what is now 27 Grassy Plain Street, and another was owned by Starr's son Eliakim, who lived at the same address. Joseph Beebe, who lived on what is now Vail Road, also owned one slave, as did Joseph Peck, who happened to be the acting minister of Bethel's Congregational Church.

Along with data that can be gathered from census and land records, available tax lists dating back to 1792 also contain substantial information. Many of these lists not only provide the names of individuals, alphabetically by last name, but also indicate their occupations. The tax lists are also useful in that "the First Ecclesiastical Society (Danbury) and the Second Ecclesiastical Society (Bethel)" are listed separately. By taking the names of individuals found in the tax records and matching them with the land they possessed, as shown by the property transfer records, we can put together an idea of who was doing what and where. For example, we find that Thaddeus Williams, who lived along Plumtrees Road, and Samuel Barnum, who lived on Walnut Hill Road, were employed as shoemakers. Phillip Wheeler of Grassy Plain Street and Edmund Beebe of Plumtrees were employed as joiners (carpenters). Bethel's sole physician was Dr. Peter Hayes, also of Grassy Plain. Benjamin Hickok, a Revolutionary War veteran, was busy in that he operated a store, a tavern and a gristmill simultaneously. Bethel possessed one tailor, one mason, three cabinetmakers and three blacksmith shops in 1793.

But the trade that would be the one most associated with Bethel over the next century and a half was, of course, hatting. In 1793, there were at least four hat shops already in operation. Thomas Taylor operated a shop just west of his house near the entrance of what is now Oakland Heights Road. This house was built before 1740 and was torn down in 1881. In a ledger kept by Taylor, one finds who his customers were and how they paid their bills. For example, "Matthew Starr, by curing leather...Hezekiah Elmor, by making 7½ lbs. of nails...Matthew Barnum by making 4 pairs of shoes... Ebenezer Whitlock, by cutting one Pig." Along with Taylor's shop, there was also the one run by Zar Dibble at what is now the southwest corner of Chestnut Street and Greenwood Avenue, Eli Hickok's shop at what is now

245 Greenwood Avenue near Farnam Hill Road, and Captain Eli Taylor's shop at what is now 51 Milwaukee Avenue.

The Danbury area even had its own newspaper, the *Farmer's Journal*, which began publication in 1790. In the pages of the paper, one can read numerous advertisements and brief notices that pertain to Bethel. An announcement dated May 30, 1791, declared, "Benjamin Hickok and Eli Mygatt have lately opened A Store of Goods in Bethel, at the house of Benjamin Hickok, Consisting of a compleat [*sic*] assortment of India and European Goods, Groceries, Crockery, all of which they will dispose of on very low terms for pay in hand: Credit will be given where the pay may be depended on; and most kinds of country produce received in payment." The house mentioned in the ad was most likely Hickok's home at what is now 2 Chestnut Street.

According to another ad, it seems Hickok and Mygatt had competition just down the road:

Nichols and Dibble Inform the Public, that they have removed their Store from Great Plain, to the parish of BETHEL, about sixty rods west of the

Benjamin Hickok and Eli Mygatt,
Have lately opened
A STORE OF GOODS,
In BETHEL, at the houfe of Benjamin Hickok,
CONSISTING of a compleat affortment of India and European Goods, Groceries, Crockery, and almoft every article in the Hard Ware line, all of which they will difpofe of on very low terms for pay in hand : Credit will be given where the pay may be depended on ; and moft kinds of country produce received in payment.
Bethel, May 30, 1791.   •   64

An advertisement placed in a 1791 issue of *The Farmer's Journal* by Benjamin Hickok and Eli Mygatt. The store being advertised was at what is now 2 Chestnut Street and was apparently a small building attached to the north side of Hickok's home.

Meeting-House, where they have on hand European, East and West-India Goods, which they are determined to sell as low for ready pay, as any Store in the county: Credit will be given where the pay may be depended upon at the time affixed. Most kinds of Country Produce, will be received in payment. Also, Old Pewter, Copper and Brass, and Public Securities at their full value. The smallest favors will be thankfully acknowledged.

Ebenezer Nichols and Zar Dibble would have had their store 990 feet (sixty rods) west of the Congregational church, where the east entrance to School Street is now. It seems their business partnership was not a successful one, for in an October issue of *The Farmer's Journal* there appears an ad reading, "The Partnership under the Firm of Nichols and Dibble Is this day dissolved by mutual agreement," but the same ad stated that the business would reemerge as Judd and Dibble.

NICHOLS & DIBBLE,

INFORM the Public, that they have removed their Store from Great-Plain, to the parish of BETHEL, about sixty rods west of the Meeting-House, where they have on hand EUROPEAN, EAST and WEST-INDIA GOODS, which they are determined to sell as low for ready pay, as any Store in the county: Credit will be given where the pay may be depended on at the time affixed. Most kinds of Country Produce, will be received in payment. Also, Old Pewter, Copper and Brass, and Public Securities at their full value. The smallest favors will be thankfully acknowledged.

☞ They want to purchase a number of PACING HORSES for Shipping.

Danbury, March 14, 1791. 53 3

A 1791 advertisement from *The Farmer's Journal*, the Danbury area's first known newspaper. The Bethel store being advertised was located near the north end of today's P.T. Barnum Square. The proprietors were Ebenezer Nichols and Zar Dibble. Their efforts were unsuccessful, and only a year and a half later they were advertising the sale of their establishment.

NEW STORE AND NEW GOODS.

THE Subscriber has removed into his New Store, and just returned from New-York, with a splendid assortment of new and fashionable fall and winter goods: among which are Blue, Black, Brown and Mixt Broad Cloths; Ladies Cloth; Casimers, Satinets, some for 50 cents per yard, Circassians of various colors, Merino Circassians, Black do., Red, Invisible Green, and Clarret colored Merino cloth; black, red and white Thibet, and Merino 4-4 to 8-4 Shawls, the GREATEST assortment ever offered in this Town, Barcelona, Flag, Pongee and Fancy silk Hdkfs; Silk Stockings some for 50 cents a pair, black, white brown and mixt worsted and cotton Stockings; Cotton and Linen table cloths, Salisbury Flannel, Furniture plaid, Bedspreads, Beaticks, Ginghams Calicoes, red, white, yellow and green Flannels; bleached and unbleached Cotton Shirtings and Sheetings, Irish Linen, Linen Cambric, Pocket Hdkfs, Ladies Cravatts a new article, belt ribins, Bead work Bags, Beads and Bead Needles, Silver Thimbles, Merino and inserting trimmings, Cotton, Linen and Bobinet Laces wide and narrow, sewing silks and twist &c., with a great variety of other articles too numerous to mention in an advertisement—All of which have been purchased at unusual low prices, and are now offered for Sale at a small advance for cash or Country produce

SETH SEELYE.

Bethel, Nov. 13th, 1832.   11f

An advertisement placed by Bethel merchant Seth Seelye in the *Danbury Gazette* in November 1832 in which he heralds his new store. Seelye built the house that later became today's Bethel Public Library, and his store was located across the street in a building that still exists as 190 Greenwood Avenue. Many old-time Bethelites will remember the location as having housed Nelson's Hardware store for many years.

So it can be seen from this brief examination of various sources that even in the 1790s Bethel was already a bustling community with a small but industrious population. Our town may have grown considerably in over two hundred years, but it would seem our present residents are as equally industrious as their forebears.

11

Bethel's Hatting Industry and Its King of Hatters

From the late 1700s until the late 1960s, hatting was Bethel's primary industry. One of the earliest-known hatters in our town was Zar Dibble, who had a hat shop near the southwest corner of Greenwood Avenue and Chestnut Street where a used car lot stands today. Another was Eli Taylor, whose home was at 51 Milwaukee Avenue, with his hat shop standing nearby. A third was Eli Hickok, whose hat shop was located behind his home at the northwest corner of Greenwood and Farnam Avenues. Yet another was Thomas Taylor, whose home and shop were located near 114 South Street, close to the entrance to Oakland Heights. A ledger kept by Bethel hatter Thomas Taylor can be found in the archives of the Connecticut State Library. The first line of the ledger reads, "December 4th, 1789—I began the hat[t]ing business—Glover Mansfield for my workman." This was quickly followed by "February 13th 1790 he left me" and next by "December 1790 I begin this business the 2nd time—Hutton Dibble for my workman."

For the most part, hatting remained a small cottage industry until after the Civil War. Most work was carried on in small shops usually on the grounds of the owner's homestead and employed a handful of workers at best. The shops were not yet factories, as they utilized no large-scale machinery but rather small hand tools made from iron and wood. Hatting also involved using a great deal of water for smoothing and shrinking animal fur into felt. Evidence suggests that seven gallons of water were required for the making

Bethel's Hatting Industry and Its King of Hatters

Above: One of Bethel's earliest houses is shown in this image from a book entitled *The Homes of our Forefathers* published in 1882. The edifice stood at 114 South Street, just east of the entrance to Oakland Heights. Thomas Taylor began his hatter's shop on the grounds of this home in 1789.

Right: An image of a nineteenth-century hatter that comes from *The Book of Trades or Library of the Useful Arts* originally published in 1807. For nearly two centuries, the manufacturing of hats served as Bethel's principal industry.

of each hat. For this reason, hat shops were usually located near a good source of water such as a river or stream, or at the very least, a reliable well.

The true golden age of hatting in Bethel took place during the 1880s. A visitor to our town would have seen evidence of the hat making business almost anywhere he turned. There were at least five establishments on Greenwood Avenue, three at P.T. Barnum Square and Main Street, three more on Nashville Road and one on South Street where the parking area for Parloa Park is today. Along with these could be found factories that specialized in the making of leather sweat bands and small silk ribbons for the inner portion of hats, hat wires that strengthened brims and provided the framework for silk hats, and box making shops that produced both cardboard

An 1850s business directory advertisement for the Bethel hat manufacturers Horace E. Hickok and Matthew W. Starr. This firm and several others in Bethel did quite well until being adversely affected by the economic panic of 1857. *Courtesy of the Danbury Museum & Historical Society.*

A circa 1880 view of the hat factory of Horace E. Hickok and Son, which was on lower Nashville Road. Shortly after the date of this photo, the company discontinued business, and the main building was made into a tenement house. It survives to the present day. *From the Clark Photo Collection, the Connecticut State Library.*

boxes for packaging and wooden boxes for shipping. Census records from the late 1800s give ample evidence that a vast number of Bethel's citizens were connected with hatting in one way or another, and those who were not had businesses that depended on the incomes generated by it. The hatting boom of the 1880s created a need for more and more workers. Luckily, there was an abundance of immigrants flocking to the northeastern United States in search of work. This population growth in turn generated a building boom, and subsequently many of Bethel's fine Victorian-style homes were erected at this time.

The arrival of the twentieth century saw a slow but gradual decrease in the demand for hats worn by both men and women. Stiff hats gave way to soft hats, and by the early 1950s, a dangerous new fashion trend was developing. Men were more and more frequently not wearing any hats at all. This new development so frightened Danbury, the "Hat Capital of the World," that the *Danbury News-Times* ran a message on the left side of its

An image from the November 23, 1887 issue of the *Danbury News* depicting the Cochran, Baird and Levi hat factory that was on the south side of lower Main Street. The factory and an adjoining one owned by George G. Durant were totally destroyed by one of Bethel's biggest fires on the afternoon of October 15, 1892.

masthead that warned: "Wear a Hat! Keep your neighbor working!" Some have blamed this change in fashion on automobiles that had lower rooflines, which made wearing a hat inconvenient. Others have attributed it to the increasing vanity of men, who did not want their carefully combed hair mussed by a hat. Some even believe the fate of hatting was sealed when President John F. Kennedy wore a top hat only briefly at his inauguration in 1961 and rarely wore a hat afterward. For whatever reason, we do know that the last operating hat factory in Bethel, the Barton Rough Hat Factory, closed its doors in 1968. This business was at 1 Main Street, where the Phineas Park apartment complex is currently situated. The vacant factory was torn down in April 1969.

When the Barton Rough Hat factory closed in 1968, the long history of Bethel hatting came to an end. During the two centuries that hat making existed in our town, many hat manufacturers came and went, but none matched the scale or output of Orrin Benedict, who rightly deserves the title "King of Bethel Hatters." Descended from James Benedict, who was one of the original settlers of Danbury in 1684, and from Hezekiah Benedict, who had his property confiscated by the state for being a Loyalist during the American Revolution, Orrin Benedict was born in Danbury on December

29, 1817. He died in Bethel on March 9, 1901, at the age of eighty-three. Benedict's obituary from the *Danbury News* of March 13, 1901, provides a glimpse of Benedict's life:

> *The death of Orrin Benedict occurred on last Saturday afternoon, at the home of his daughter, Mrs. Theodore Ferry in Bethel, where Mr. Benedict resided. Mr. Benedict, who was for many years before his retirement from business one of the leading manufacturers of Bethel, and one of the best known men in this section of the state, had been ill about five weeks with a complication of diseases.*
>
> *Mr. Benedict was a native of Danbury, having been born in this town in 1817. When seventeen years old, he was apprenticed to learn the hatter's trade in the factory of Starr Hoyt, then a well-known Danbury establishment. "When he was twenty-four years old, Mr. Benedict began the manufacture of hats in his own factory. He began in a small way, but in a few years was the owner of large establishments in Bethel and New York City, and was counted one of the most successful manufacturers of hats in his time." In October 1840, Mr. Benedict married Julia Maria Starr, of*

A circa 1918 view of lower South Street, which was one of Bethel's most fashionable addresses, being home to many of the town's wealthiest hat manufacturers.

Danbury, the daughter of Hugh and Anna Starr. Mr. Benedict had been for more than fifty years a member of the Episcopal Church of Bethel. He served at one time as a selectman of Danbury and in 1868 represented Danbury in the legislature. In 1890 and 1891 he represented Bethel in the legislature. He was a mason and an Odd Fellow. Mr. Benedict was greatly respected by the people of his town and was counted as an honest and upright citizen, a man of marked ability in the business world and was regarded by hundreds as a staunch and loyal friend. His death will be a distinct loss to Bethel.

Orrin Benedict's home stood on the present site of a service station and car wash located just to the east of the Sycamore Drive-In restaurant on Greenwood Avenue. The house was a large Italianate-style mansion built in the mid-1800s that sat on a hill with a commanding view. The hill was subsequently excavated in the 1940s to make way for the present commercial buildings that now occupy what was once known

A 1909 postcard view of the Pine Tree Inn, which stood close to the present-day Sycamore Drive-In restaurant on Greenwood Avenue. The inn was originally built as an Italianate-style villa that served as the home of Orrin Benedict, a prominent hat manufacturer of the nineteenth century.

as "Benedict's Corner." After Benedict's death, his home was used as a hotel called the Pine Tree Inn. Prior to being demolished, the house was abandoned for a long while, and according to the 1955 Bethel centennial booklet, "It was a brave boy, even for a Grassy Plainer, who would dare enter it after dark." Before the Grassy Plain District was annexed to Bethel in 1869, Benedict's home was actually in Danbury, and his hat factory, which was just across the street on the site of the present Burger King restaurant and Bethel Cinema, was in Bethel. What remained of Benedict's factory was destroyed by fire on May 16, 1965. In its heyday, the factory employed well over one hundred workers and produced several thousand hats a week.

Orrin Benedict is buried along with several other members of his immediate family in the Center Cemetery on South Street. He has the honor of possessing the cemetery's tallest monument, and its location provides a

This large hat factory stood near the intersection of Grand Street and Dimond Avenue, and at the time of this photo, taken in the 1880s, the facility was operated under the firm name of Burns and Schoonmaker. *From the Clark Photo Collection, the Connecticut State Library.*

This postcard dates from about 1915 and shows the large Baird Unteidt hat factory which stood on lower Main Street on the site of the present Phineas Park apartment complex. The factory was torn down in April 1969.

pleasant view that looks out over downtown Bethel. Although wealthy and influential, Benedict's obituary most emphasized that he was regarded as an honest and upright citizen and a staunch and loyal friend, which is certainly the best manner in which anyone could ask to be remembered.

12

Comb Making in Bethel

B ethel's long connection with the hatting industry is well known to many, but there was another type of manufacturing that rivaled and even eclipsed hatting for a short period in the early nineteenth century: comb making. The combs of the early 1800s were of a different sort than what we are accustomed to using today. These were primarily ornamental combs used by women of fashion to keep their tresses in place and were not made of today's unbreakable plastic but rather of cow horn. The first logical question regarding the art of comb making would have to be: "How does one go about creating a comb from a cow's horn?" The answer can be found in a book first published in 1804 under the title of *The Book of Trades, or Library of the Useful Arts*. The book's fifth chapter is entitled "The Comb-Maker" and provides an interesting look at a craft that seems to have arrived in the Danbury area about 1805, only a year after the work's initial publication:

> *Bullocks'* [young bull, ox, steer] *horns are thus prepared in order to manufacture combs: the tips are first sawn off: they are then held in the flame of a wood fire; this is called roasting, by which they become nearly as soft as leather. While in that state, they are slit open on one side, and pressed in a machine between two iron plates; they are then plunged into a trough of water, which they come out hard and flat.*

The comb-maker now saws them into lengths according to the size combs he wants. To cut the teeth, each piece is fixed in a tool called a clam. The comb-maker sits on a triangular sort of stool to do his work, and under him is placed the clam that holds the horn, ivory, & .etc. that is to be formed into a comb. The teeth are cut with a fine saw, or rather a pair of saws and they are finished with a file. A coarser file called a rasp is used to reduce the horn to a proper thickness; and when the combs are made, they are polished with charcoal and water, and receive their last finish with powder of rotten-stone (limestone).

As this work was originally published in London, England, there may have been some variation in American methods. An article published in the *Danbury News* in June 1875 provided the recollections of Ammon T. Peck,

An early image of a comb maker from *The Book of Trades or Library of the Useful Arts* originally published in 1807. Comb making was once one of Bethel's primary industries, with over twenty different comb shops scattered throughout the area.

who was born in Bethel and was involved in the comb making business for many years. His account of the comb making process has many similarities with that of the British description:

In most of the shops, the occupants were at work as follows: A lad scraping horns, the boss sawing them up on a bucksaw blade, one marking out plates so as to get all the stock into combs of the largest size; two or three jours [journeymen] making the plates into combs, mostly two to each plate by a process called "trimming"; one or two rubbing and polishing the teeth and backs; a girl steaming, with a boy to help wash off; a man, often times a woman, bending the combs to fit the head of the wearers.

Generally, the combs, after bending, were taken to the house to be wiped and rubbed clean and packed in "dozen bunches" for market.

Comb making in Bethel is also chronicled in an 1881 work entitled *History of Fairfield County* published by D. Hamilton Hurd. An article contributed by Bethel native Dr. George Benedict provides the following information: "Fifty years and more ago the most prominent manufacturing interests in Bethel were comb-making and hatting, and perhaps the former was even more prominent than the latter. But the comb-makers are among the things that were. There is nothing done at the business in town now." Yet within the writer's recollection, there were a number of firms and individuals who carried on an extensive business:

In Elmwood District, Mr. Azariel Smith had a large factory which was surmounted by a cupola containing a bell. It depended upon a small stream for its power, but for its time was a large concern. It stood near the house of James P. Ridge. The factory was located just east of the intersection of Dodgingtown Road and Taylor Road, on the north side of the road. Mr. Charles Smith also had a shop in the same district a little east of the one just mentioned, nearly opposite the house formerly belonging to the late Joseph Taylor, Esq. The factory of Mr. A. Smith was destroyed by fire between forty and fifty years ago.

In Plumtrees, the firm of Charles and Horace Couch did for many years a large business. The building now known as Bartow's saw and cider mills was built by the brothers Couch for comb-making purposes. [The location just mentioned is on Walnut Hill Road near the point where it is met by Taylor Road. The saw and cider mill was on the west side of the small bridge that crosses the brook, and a gristmill was on the east side, both making use of the available water power.] *Charles Barnum also built a shop near the old factory, and for a number of years carried on the business. This was afterwards owned by Asahel Dunning and used as a hat shop.* [This shop was located again along the same stream, but this time the spot described is diagonally across the street from the old Plumtrees Schoolhouse in a northeasterly direction.] *Here were others, belonging to different members of the Williams family, in the near vicinity,* [Plumtrees Road near Walnut Hill Road] *and others in the village. There were also several early shops on Codfish Hill Road and the nearby portion of Old Hawleyville Road. Of all kinds of factories and shops for the manufacture of combs, in 1840 there were not less than twenty.*

The comb making business seems to have reached its peak in our area between 1820 and 1850. The federal census of 1850 shows thirty-three individuals in Danbury and Bethel who listed their occupations as that of comb maker. Their livelihood would soon be curtailed. According to Bailey's *History of Danbury* (1896), "In 1852 the business died out, mainly because the comb-makers in Massachusetts combined their capital and skilled labor and killed off the small manufacturers in other parts of the country." Although its run was short-lived, for a while comb making was carried out by a great portion of Bethel's populace, especially when hatting was slow or in between

An 1847 want ad placed in the *Danbury Times* by Silliman B. Peck relating to Bethel's comb making. From about 1810 up until as late as 1876, the making of women's ornamental hair combs from cow horn was an important industry in town. Comb shops could also be found in Danbury, Newtown and Brookfield.

growing seasons. Even P.T. Barnum recalled how he had "scraped horns for 10 cents per hundred" for a relative, Daniel Barnum, who operated a comb shop in the center of town.

Twenty years ago, I attended an antiques show in Stamford and amazingly, while browsing among the thousands of objects on display, discovered a small cow horn comb with a tag that read: "This cow-horn comb was made in Bethel, CT. over one hundred years ago." The dealer could only remember that she had purchased the comb from an elderly man in Bethel and that the comb had been handed down through his family. Needless to say, the comb now has a new owner in its old hometown.

13

Bethel's Cemeteries

Where the Founders Are on File

M ost people probably think that wandering around in an old cemetery is a bit morbid or, at best, a bit strange. But for anyone who wishes to commune with those who came before us and helped give us the town we have today, there is no better place to be than in one of our old burying grounds. They are all there: the great and the not so great, the influential and the obscure, the rich and the poor, the old and the very young. All of them arranged neatly in straight rows, almost as if they had been inserted into a sort of filing cabinet for the departed. Before you can experience any of these ancient necropolises, you have to search out their locations. Bethel possesses six formal cemeteries. There is the Congregational Cemetery, traditionally known as the "Old Burying Ground," beside the Congregational church on Main Street. This is the town's earliest final resting place, with the oldest legible stone dating back to 1765. There is the Center Cemetery on South Street that dates to 1847. It was created when the one on Main Street was forced to hang out a No Vacancy sign. There is also St. Mary's Cemetery on Route 53, which was first put into use in 1891. Its creation reflected the growing number of Roman Catholics who had made Bethel their home by that time.

Another, Elmwood Cemetery, on Route 302, was originally established as a family burial ground by the Andrews family in 1845. The Wolfpits Cemetery is on Sunset Hill Road and dates to the year 1815. It was established by the first five families to live in the area around Sunset Hill. A great number of the

The Center Cemetery Civil War monument as it looked in about the year 1911. The Center Cemetery was created in 1847, and the granite monument was dedicated in 1892.

individuals buried there are members of the Hoyt family. Finally, the Stony Hill Cemetery is on a winding portion of Walnut Hill Road, now surrounded by the Chimney Heights housing development. This burying ground was established by the Dibble family as early as 1793, and volume one of the Danbury town records states that at a meeting held on December 20, 1802, "Col. Eli Mygatt was appointed to receive a release of the ground given by Samuel Dibble for a Burying ground place at Stony Hill in behalf of the town."

Today, few individuals notice these ancient places of interment as they speed by them in their automobiles. Few realize the tremendous examples of art and craftsmanship that lie just a few feet from the roadway, slowly decaying but still defiant to the passing years. The truly ancient stones are often adorned with winged angel heads or weeping willows standing close alongside funeral urns; those that date from the latter half of the nineteenth century are often topped by a downcast woman in a Grecian gown, or in the case of a small child, the figure of a lamb is often employed to symbolize death that came before its time.

The carvings or statuary of the graves can often be outdone by the inscriptions found on the faces of the headstones. Some provide information on the character of the deceased individual, such as in the case of Captain Ebenezer Hickok, who is buried in the Congregational Cemetery. His inscription reads, "Here lies buried the body of Captain Ebenezer Hickok who departed this life July 8th A.D.

1774 in the 83rd Year of his Age. He was for many Years a Deacon in the Church of Bethel a principal Pillar in that Church and Society and an Ornament to the Christian Religion—The memory of the Righteous is blessed." The fact that Captain Hickok had donated the land for the Congregational church and its cemetery may have helped to inspire this glowing epitaph.

Along with brief biographies, warnings also appear on some stones, still speaking to us across the ages. One, found in the Congregational Cemetery, is of particular interest: "Reader beware as you pass by, as you are now so once was I, As I am now so you must be, Prepare for death and follow me." (A jokester once scratched this retort on a gravestone with an identical inscription: "To follow you I'd be content, If only I knew which way you went!") The most compelling reason of all to visit any of Bethel's ancient burying grounds is to remember, to remember and wonder at those who settled our area and all they must have gone through. How did they survive when this region was simply wilderness? How did they clear the forests, build homes, create roads and establish churches and schools? How did they survive the harsh winters and the cruel summers? How did they deal with death that came all too frequently from illnesses and diseases we no longer fear? Somehow they not only survived but also triumphed. They persevered, hoping that through their struggle, those who came after might have it a bit easier and a bit better. We do, but it is a direct result of the foundation that was laid down by those brave souls who now lie nearly forgotten beneath the green grass of the cemeteries scattered throughout our town.

The next time you find yourself whizzing by one these spots at high speeds in your air-conditioned car, reflect on those who carved out the road you're traveling on or built the church to which you are speeding. Or better yet, pull your car over to the side of the road and take a few minutes to look over the names you can still make out on some of the headstones. Visit for just a short time with Thaddeus Starr, who nearly lost his sight as a result of contracting smallpox while fighting in the American Revolution. Or take time out to gaze upon the grave of a young Civil War soldier named Irenaeus P. Woodman, who was just seventeen when he died from wounds received at the Battle of Chancellorsville, Virginia. Or linger for just a short while to view the graves of the families whose names are now only remembered by way of the designations given to our streets: the Benedicts, the Weeds, the Vails, the Hoyts or the Judds. They are all there. But if you do stop at these sites, act with reverence, and remember the caveat of that old headstone, "As you are now so once was I."

14
Stony Hill's First Historian

A mong the multitude of closely packed stacks lodged in the Connecticut State Library in Hartford is an old manuscript originally placed there in 1921. The thick, photocopied packet is made up of negative photostatic images rather than positive ones, so its pages appear black while its lettering is white. Subsequently, its legibility is quite poor. The formal title of the work is "List of Old Houses One Hundred Years Old or Over Standing February, 1921 in the Vicinity of Danbury, Connecticut." The author's name appears below the title as Henry B. Betts of Danbury, Connecticut. Betts was a farmer by trade, but he was also someone who was intensely inquisitive about local history. During his lifetime, he amassed a tremendous amount of information regarding the early settlement of both Danbury and Bethel, with his greatest interest being his own Stony Hill area, which straddled portions of both towns. The historical record he compiled is somewhat difficult to read at times, as it switches back and forth from narrative to simple notes that often do not take the form of full sentences or contain any punctuation. Despite these shortcomings, Betts preserved information that proves invaluable to anyone researching this area today, and subsequently it is easy to say that Betts therefore qualifies as Stony Hill's first historian.

Henry Benjamin Betts was born November 9, 1873, in Wilton, Connecticut, the son of Elijah Betts (b. March 27, 1840; d. September 28, 1878) and Mary Viola (Knapp) Betts (b. January 13, 1853; d. February

25, 1930). On October 2, 1901, Henry Betts married Jessie C. Beers, the daughter of James Clark Beers of Danbury. The marriage would produce one child, Lois Wildey Betts, who was born on August 30, 1911. Later in life, Betts would give up farming for the hatter's trade, working for the Frank H. Lee Hat Company in Danbury for twenty-five years. The family lived in a house that was originally the home of Henry Holt Knapp, Betts's maternal grandfather, who continued to live with them until his death in 1913. The Betts home then included several acres and served as a dairy farm nicknamed "Pocono Farm." The house was on what is now U.S. Route 6 on the Danbury-Bethel town line and for many years afterward served as the "1848 House" restaurant. The house, barns and outbuildings were demolished in 2002 to make way for a Volvo auto dealership

Henry Betts apparently became interested in the history of Danbury and the Stony Hill area in particular, at a very young age. Betts mentions interviewing Colonel Nathan B. Dibble, who died as early as 1891. At that time, Betts would have been only eighteen years old. His interest may have stemmed from the fact that his maternal great-grandmother, Amelia (Benedict) Knapp, was of the original Benedict family that helped establish Danbury in 1684. The Knapp family was also among Danbury's earliest families, settling there before 1697. Betts may have grown up hearing stories of his ancestors' exploits and become interested in learning more.

By 1921, Henry Betts had assembled a vast collection of facts concerning the early settlers of Stony Hill—in many cases, gaining them from the last descendants of families who had lived in the area for over two hundred years. In his work, Betts noted that nearly all the families of Stony Hill seemed to have been related in the time between the American Revolution and the Civil War. This fact made it infinitely easier to trace the genealogies and land transfers of these early settlers, and yet some information on the area's initial pioneers may never be known. Tracing the earliest history of Danbury is particularly hampered by the fact that the town's land records were destroyed when British troops burned Danbury in April 1777. Brookfield, which was made up of land taken from Danbury, Newtown and New Milford and which would not be set off as a separate town until 1788, and Bethel, which would not be set off until 1855, also lost records of early land transfers as a result of the British attack.

When Betts died on March 5, 1953, Danbury and Bethel were undergoing a time of unparalleled growth. He had lived to see the simple dirt road that

An early 1950s postcard view of a Stony Hill farm located on Old Hawleyville Road that was known as "Upwey." The farm was then owned by prominent New York banker and noted book collector Alfred Corey Howell. The driveway of the farmhouse in the foreground was later widened to create a street, and the house today is designated as 1 Kristy Drive.

passed in front of his home become a major thoroughfare, and if he had lived less than a decade longer, he would have seen U.S. Interstate 84 pass behind his property and the construction of an entrance ramp running close to where his cattle barns had stood. By 1953, the families of the Stony Hill area were also changing. The Benedicts, Beebes, Vails and Weeds, who had owned the area's farmland, were dying off, and their farms were being turned into housing developments for the couples who would generate the baby boom of the postwar era. The hatting industry in which Betts worked for a quarter of a century, Danbury's major employer since the 1700s, was then in a state of decline, which ended with the last of its hat factories closing in 1987. In short, Danbury was changing from a rural farming community to a suburban satellite of New York City. Those who were now calling Danbury home had no ties to, and little knowledge of, the area's past. In light of these changes, it was fortunate that Henry Betts wrote down his findings when he did. Had he not, a vital link with the past might have been lost forever.

Betts's 1921 manuscript "List of Old Houses" contains fifty-five different entries providing information on houses and other places of interest, with a

An aerial view of the eastern portion of Stony Hill that dates from about 1957. In the lower portion of the photo can be seen both Redwood Drive and Old Hawleyville Road. Connecticut Route 6 extends west toward Danbury in the upper right as it passes the Stony Hill Inn.

good portion of them lying within the boundaries of Bethel. Along with producing his own historical piece, Betts compiled information on historic houses in the early 1920s for a group known as the Colonial Dames of Connecticut in preparation for a book entitled *Old Houses of Connecticut*. The work was authored by Bertha Chadwick Trowbridge and appeared first in 1923, but unfortunately it did not feature any of the houses Betts had researched in the Stony Hill area. Some of the more intriguing entries from both works are provided below, precisely as Betts recorded them in his notes, though in some cases additional information is provided for clarity. Statements found within parentheses indicate marginalia added later by Betts.

THE MAJOR DIKEMAN PLACE

The house described in the following account is today identified as 35 Hawleyville Road. The date of construction that has long been ascribed to the home is 1765. It is undoubtedly one of the oldest, if not the oldest house, in the Stony Hill district.

> *Old Major Dikeman Place—Stony Hill, Bethel, Conn. On Danbury and Hawleyville Highway which was the original Danbury and Newtown Highway in Revolutionary Times. Compiled by Henry B. Betts, April 26, 1915.*
>
> *House built for Nathaniel Benedict—Commonly known as Major Dikeman Place—Now owned by Aldrich A. Wohlken situated in the town of Bethel County of Fairfield built before the Revolutionary War—The original settler to own the land was probably Nathaniel Benedict.*
>
> *Location—House faces north point of the compass and is set back 40 feet from the Danbury & Hawleyville Rd. There are remains of a garden in the rear.*
>
> *Danbury Probate records—Nathaniel Benedict b. about 1680—made will Jan. 19, 1767, Probated Dec. 1, 1767.*
>
> *Fifty Acres—This seems to be the land where the house stands.*
>
> *Bounded—East & North by highway, West part by John McLean's land, West and North—by part Jakin Benedict.*
>
> *West—part by highway, East & South—part by Elijah wood's land and part southerly by highway.*

The area described above seems to have contained all the land that is found today within the boundaries of Hawleyville Road on the north, Old Hawleyville Road on the east, Route 6 on the south and McNeil Road on the west.

Betts's notes later relate how the heirs of Nathaniel Benedict named Thomas and Ethel Benedict sold the house and fourteen acres to Major Dikeman on February 16, 1839, as indicated by *Danbury Land Records*, volume thirty-one. Betts concludes his account by stating that "Major Dikeman died fall of 1890 and his son George d. 1893 whose widow & sons sold it to present owners about 1908."

Genealogical records state that Major Dikeman actually died at the age of eighty-five on November 15, 1890, and that George B. Dikeman died on July 20, 1895, at the age of fifty-six. Both are buried in the Stony Hill Cemetery on Walnut Hill Road. The owner at the time of Betts's research in 1915 was Aldrich A. Wohlken, whose occupation is listed as that of carpenter in the city directories of the period.

Peter O'Brien House

Betts also describes another old home in his "List of Houses" that no longer exists but once stood on the north side of Hawleyville Road not far from its intersection with Vail Road. Here he liberally borrows from Bailey's *History of Danbury*:

> *Peter O'Brien House at "old town place"—History (of) Danbury p. 212—Peter O'Brien was Danbury's first Irishman coming to Danbury about 1825.* [Danbury land records show that O'Brien first purchased land in Danbury on March 14, 1826.] *He located himself in Stony Hill just east of the school house and put up a genuine shanty made of stone clay and turf with a barrel for a chimney and was one of Danbury's greatest attractions in these days. He kept a cow, pigs and chickens that were always seen hovering about the door unless occasionally when Mrs. O' Brien drove them away—"when asked how he came over from Ireland" said "Faith and I came over in a horse cart." No other data is available but must have been east of "Friendship Farm."*

Friendship Farm was the name given to a house and accompanying property that was situated at today's 4 Hawleyville Road. At the time of Betts's research, the house was owned by Mrs. Sara Libby Carson of New York City. This house had its property bisected by the construction of Interstate 84 in 1961. O'Brien's house would have been on the north side of Hawleyville Road close to its intersection with Vail Road.

The Peter O'Brien mentioned here was also described by P.T. Barnum in his original autobiography published in 1854. In speaking of how he had worked at his father's store as a boy, Barnum states that "one of the customers at our store was an Irishman named Peter O'Brien, a small farmer in one of the districts several miles north of Bethel." Barnum goes on to relate how O'Brien used his "droll mother-wit" to trick a fellow townsmen into buying a blind dog, after promising that the dog would "chase anything that he'd see, and watch all that you would show him." Bailey's *History of Danbury* provides roughly the same account but includes the name of the individual duped by O'Brien.

OLD INDIAN CAMP

In another portion of "List of Old Houses," Betts makes reference to an "Old Indian Camp." He states that it was located

> *near Danbury and Bethel town lines, south of Danbury and Newtown state trunkline* [today's Route 6] *with small burial place nearby, easterly of a spring on highway, southwest* [actually northeast] *of where town division line leaves center of highway and turns west towards East Swamp Brook and division line of Stony Hill and Plumtrees Districts in Bethel. Several round paved places show locations of old Indian Wigwams. Said to have been an old Indian trail through here north and south.*

In carefully looking over the notes Betts scribbled in 1920 on an 1889 geological survey map of the area, one can determine that the spot being described would today be in the Chimney Heights area on the north side of Adams Drive, near its junction with Benedict Road. Due to development, any trace of the campground has probably long since been erased.

Elsewhere in the same work, Betts imparts one other interesting tidbit relating to Native Americans in the Stony Hill area. His mother was born Mary Viola Knapp and was descended from one of the area's earliest families. Betts recounts a tale involving one of his mother's family ancestors named Mercy Knapp, who was born in 1727 and died on May 15, 1811. She married Lieutenant Thomas Benedict in about the year 1750 and moved to the Stony Hill area.

> *It is said that Lieutenant Thomas Benedict's wife—Mercy Knapp who was born on South St. Danbury was nearly scared to death sometimes*

An early 1950s postcard view of Nugent's Modern Cabins and Tourist Home, which stood for many years along the north side of Route 6 just east of the Stony Hill Inn.

when she first came to this place as there were some Indians still running around—some—probably they were the "south tribe" of Schaticokes or "Beaver Brook Indians"—who had headquarters near Beaver Brook Mt.—the north tribe being at Kent, Conn. When her husband was away after dark she would go to meet him[,] then if she heard a noise be afraid it wasn't him and possibly an Indian [then] would run back again, etc. A good many times Indians came and looked through the windows in the evenings if the curtains were not let down or shutters closed—Indian fashion[,] shading their face with a hand held up on each side. These were some of the "Good Old Times."

These are just three snippets of Stony Hill lore that Henry Betts chronicled in his work. He was far ahead of his time in his appreciation of both local history and colonial architecture. It is sad to note that many of the homes and sites he diligently researched survived from the eighteenth century up until his own time in the 1920s, only to be obliterated in the closing decades of the twentieth century.

15

The Plumtrees Schoolhouse

It is a cheerful survivor from a simpler era that has somehow withstood the tidal wave of time that has swept away all traces of the world it once knew. It was home to the laughter and tears, the songs and shouts and lessons and games of energetic young occupants for over a century, and has remained so revered by its students and supporters that they have staunchly prevented it from passing away. In short, there is something quite special about the little white Plumtrees Schoolhouse.

There has been an area known as Plumtrees even longer than there has been a place called Bethel. Area probate records that survived the burning of Danbury by the British in 1777 contain its name. The label retains its ancient form and spelling, which combines two words into one, and is devoid of the letter "b." Early on, the residents of Plumtrees, though not great in numbers, saw the need for schools. Upon the brittle pages of church records belonging to the Bethel Congregational Church can be found an entry making this clear:

> *At a Societies Meeting Legally Warned held in Bethel Parrish in Danbury on ye 28th Day of December 1768 Decn John Benedict was chosen Moderator at sd meeting ye question was put whether ye society would have three Districts of Schools in sd Society Bounded in ye following Manner viz Beginning at ye meeting house tacking all upon plumtree Road and upon*

ye road out by Capt Bebe to Newtown line to be ye Northern district and all Eastward of above sd road from ye top of hoyts hill to be ye Eastward District and ye remaining part of ye society to be ye Western District Voted in the affirmative.

The Captain Beebe referenced was Lemuel Beebe, who operated a gristmill on Plumtrees Brook and lived in small saltbox-style house that still stands just a short distance from the school, on the opposite side of the road.

In January 1769, the Connecticut Colonial Assembly granted the society of Bethel, which had been set off as a separate parish from the First Ecclesiastical Society of Danbury just ten years earlier, the right to its portion of a school fund that had originally been set up in 1732, and to a second fund left by Danbury's Comfort Starr following his death in 1763. The Bethel Society's members met on January 6, 1769, and voted to create a new school district specifically for "Stoney Hill." Twenty-three years later, the society decided to expand the size of the Stony Hill district and to redefine its boundary with the Plumtrees school district: "At a societies meeting Legally warned & held at the meeting house in Bethel on Tuesday the 25th of Dec 1792 The society By vote Divide the Northern District of Schools into two—the line to run from the Road across East Swamp to Newtown—Line taking in Thaddeus Starr & David Barnum to the north part." (As the date of this meeting indicates, our Puritan ancestors did not celebrate Christmas as an official holiday.)

The earliest students of Plumtrees may have attended classes that were conducted in a private home, but recent investigation shows that Plumtrees did have its own schoolhouse as early as the late 1700s. In fact, it is now clear that at least two different Plumtrees school buildings preceded the now familiar one begun in 1867. The evidence comes from an article first published in the *Bethel Press* and reprinted in the *Newtown Bee* on March 28, 1878. The article appears under the simple heading of "Plumtrees." It begins:

To every one acquainted with Plumtrees, a familiar object is the little old wagon house of Mr. Rufus L. Couch, standing on the hill just above Mr. H.H. Baird's "old red house." It is not a thing of beauty, but rather an object of veneration. It's [sic] walls are not ivy-mantled, neither is it's roof moss-grown. It stands bare and gray on the hill where it has stood for a

century. That was the old-time schoolhouse. There the Plumtrees lads and
lasses of other generations were initiated into the mysteries of A.B.C. There
they were introduced to the genial Daboll and good old Lindly Murray of
blessed memory.

The spot being described is today's Walnut Hill Road near its connection
with Shelter Rock Road. The Rufus L. Couch who is described as the old
school's owner lived at what is now 32 Walnut Hill Road. Bethel maps
of 1856, 1858 and 1867 all agree on this. (Later, the *Bee* article mentions
that Couch himself was a graduate of the school.) The "old red house"
mentioned is today's 28 Walnut Hill Road, a house that sits geographically
below the previously mentioned site. There is a good likelihood that a small
addition situated at the southwest corner of the house at 32 Walnut Hill
Road is in fact the old schoolhouse described. It is probable that after initially
being converted to a wagon house, it was later moved a short distance and
connected to the nearby home for additional living space. Despite being
annexed to the neighboring dwelling and re-sided, the structure retains the
size and shape of a typical early American schoolhouse. (Verification of the
location and ownership of these buildings can be found in the *Bethel Land
Records*, volume five.) The reference to "Daboll" and "Lindly Murray" relates
to the authors of two textbooks widely used in our nation's public schools of
the early 1800s. Nathan Daboll produced the *Nathan Daboll Arithmetic Book* in
1821, and Lindley Murray published his *English Grammar* book in 1795.

The *Bee*'s article continues by giving a detailed account of what it was like
to attend this first Plumtrees School. The contents paint an intimate portrait
of the nature of New England education in the early 1800s:

The bright little Plum-tree blossoms of to-day the arophetic [prophetic]
fruit of the next generation, who attend school in the present commodious
and pleasant schoolhouse, have but little conception of the schoolhouse of
that old day. It was in no sense a Yale College or a Harvard. The main
room was perhaps twelve by fifteen feet, with stationary writing tables or
"forms" built against the walls running around on the sides and one end.
The seats were long benches without backs, made of oak planks or "slabs,"
the softest being selected. In the ends of these planks auger holes were bored
at a proper angle into which long pegs were driven for legs. These benches

were placed before the writing tables in a line around the room. On these benches were seated the older boys and girls "graded" according to age and advancement. When seated they formed a kind of hollow square. Within this square smaller benches of the same soft material and similar construction were placed for the younger—the "sophomores and freshmen." On these oaken benches the little ones had to sit for hours with no support for their backs. By long years of seasoning these slabs had become almost as hard as stone and by constant friction as smooth as polished marble. The teacher's desk was placed towards the end of this hollow square, and with one chair for the teacher, completed the furniture of the room. Here the teacher presided, ruled and feruled. There were no maps on the walls, no blackboards, no globes. The books were dry and hard.

The house had a large stone chimney, and an ample fire-place which in the earlier days was the only means of warming the room. In its later days it enjoyed the luxury of a "box" stove.

The account goes on to relate the names of many Plumtrees residents who attended the school. Most of the individuals identified were born between the 1790s and 1820, indicating that the school was in use quite early. The article states in the first paragraph that the schoolhouse had stood "for a century." If this were taken literally, the building may have been constructed as early as 1778, if not earlier.

In the final portion of this remarkable memoir, the author makes clear that Plumtrees had indeed utilized three different schoolhouses over time: "Many years ago a new school house was built near the residence of Mr. Abram Hoyt, the old one being too limited to answer the demands of the district. That in turn did not accommodate all, and the present commodious house was built a few years ago. Educational matters in Plumtrees have kept pace with the times."

The aforementioned second Plumtrees Schoolhouse stood directly across the street from the present one, near the northeast corner of Taylor Road and Plumtrees Road and is clearly labeled on the 1867 *Beers' Atlas of Fairfield County* map of Bethel. On the same map, at a short distance to the northwest, is a dwelling labeled "A. Hoyt" for Abram Hoyt, which directly corresponds with the account. That house today is identified as 75 Taylor Road. *Danbury Land Records* show that land for the second school was purchased on November 8,

1830, as indicated in a transfer of property from Asel Starr to Ira Barnum from the "Committee of the Plumtrees School District." The property is conveyed to "Ira Barnum committee as aforesaid and his successor in office for the purpose of building a school house, a certain or parcel of land situated in said Danbury in Plumtrees District containing about four rods more or less it being thirty feet on the East & West line and twenty four feet on the North and South line, Bounded North & West by my other land, East by Abel Beebe wife's land, South by highway." The property was sold for the recorded price of one dollar. On September 11, 1848, a second purchase was made transferring land from Asel (actually Ashael) Dunning to George B. Crofut. This acquisition was made presumably to expand the size of the school's property and was located to the rear of the schoolhouse and in front of Plumtrees Brook.

This second school building was replaced after 1867, but its later fate is not entirely certain. When the Shepaug Railroad's branch line was put through in 1872, it ran perilously close to the back of the structure. However, judging by an 1889 geological survey map of the area that uses small black squares to indicate existing buildings, the second schoolhouse survived the construction of the nearby tracks. It is possible that at some ensuing time the edifice was moved to a new location just a short distance away. A small dwelling house that stood for many years in the area across the street from 73 Rockwell Road had a size and shape reminiscent of a one-room schoolhouse. The building was demolished within the last twenty years, but photographs survive. More investigation needs to be done regarding this theory.

During the decade that would see the nation torn apart by civil war, Bethel's population would grow by exactly 600 residents, increasing from 1,711 in 1860 to 2,311 by 1870. In 1867, this population spike began to place pressure on the residents of Plumtrees to provide a larger school for their children. A solution would soon be found. A Bethel land deed dated October 1, 1867 states:

> *I, Eliza Benedict, of the town of Bethel Fairfield County and State of Connecticut for the consideration of One Hundred and Ten Dollars received to my full satisfaction of the Plumtrees School District by Levi Clark, Committee of Said District—do give, grant, bargain sell and confirm unto the said School District for School purposes and none other purpose, one certain piece of Land situated in Bethel, at Plumtrees so called, Bounded on*

the North and West by Highway, on the East and South by my other Land and Highway, containing about one half acre, be the same, more or less.

The next portion of the document would cause considerable consternation at various times from the point of its conception up until and including the present day: "The conditions of this deed are now these, that if any thing occurs, that the above described property is not occupied as site for a School House, it shall revert back to me, or my heirs at Law, before being disposed of, to be used for any other purpose." Benedict's proviso may have been inspired by seeing the previous schoolhouse site created and given up all within her lifetime. Despite the stipulations, the citizens of the Plumtrees school district now had land on which to construct a new school, and it is presumed that within the following year, with numerous hands pitching in, the task was completed. As the property was obtained in October 1867, it is reasonable to assume that the school was probably not completed and occupied until at least 1868.

Eliza Benedict, the benefactress of the new school grounds, was what would have been referred to in those days as a "spinster" in that she never married. Aged forty-seven at the time she sold the future school site, she was born on April 11, 1820, to John Benedict of Plumtrees and Betsey Leavenworth Benedict of Monroe. She was one of three children, having two younger brothers: Andrew, born in 1822, and George, born in 1824. The family lived on a farm at what is now 73 Plumtrees Road, just up the road and in sight of the present schoolhouse property. Her brothers would

The Plumtrees one-room schoolhouse as it appeared in the early 1900s. The school has roots that date back to 1867 and did not cease service until 1970. This image shows the school before its clapboard siding was covered with shake shingles. *Courtesy of Ruth Stevenson MacGill.*

both become quite successful, with Andrew becoming a businessman in both Bethel and New York City and George becoming a prominent doctor who had graduated from both Yale College and Yale Medical School. Andrew had also taught school in the earlier Plumtrees School and was remembered as a gentle taskmaster. It was said of him, "His government was of a persuasive nature in school; a kind word often did better than the use of the ferule." Eliza herself was very active in the Congregational Church and taught its Sunday school in Plumtrees for many years. In the later years of performing this service, she taught her students in the schoolhouse set up on the very ground she had provided.

An interesting reminiscence, told years after her death, gives us a glimpse into the character of Eliza Benedict. Her nephew George would spend all of his boyhood vacations from school at the old family home at 73 Rockwell Road. Beginning in 1871, the Shepaug Railway ran a branch line from the center of Bethel to Hawleyville in Newtown. The railroad tracks ran directly behind the Benedict homestead at a distance of approximately five hundred feet. In later life, when her nephew would bring his family to visit from their home in Quincy, Massachusetts, a humorous method was employed to shorten the group's railroad travel time. Her nephew would recall: "The children always watched eagerly from the train for a sight which never failed to greet them. It was the waving of a big white tablecloth that Aunt Eliza had run out to the yard with. As though by magic, the train slowed down in the meadow, and stopped just long enough to let this excited family tumble out." Later in the account, it is revealed that a "bribe" of cigars for the engineer was the true incentive for this unscheduled stop.

When Eliza Benedict died on October 7, 1899, at the age of seventy-seven, the *Newtown Bee* stated, "The deceased was a lifelong resident of Plumtrees school district and has spent the greater part of her life, nearly eighty years, in her late home, which she inherited from her late father and mother, John and Betsey Benedict. Miss Benedict was for over a half century a useful and constant member of the Congregational church." Dying just before the dawn of the new century, Benedict could have little realized how her provision of land would help to positively affect generations to come.

As commodious as the new school at the corner of Taylor and Plumtrees Roads was, population growth in the Plumtrees district would soon once again dictate that provisions be made for additional classroom space. A short notice in the *Danbury News* of July 12, 1882, placed under the heading of "Passing Events In Plumtrees" states, "Work has commenced on the foundation of the new addition to the school-house. There has been an increase of fourteen to the number of children under sixteen years of age, in two months." And another piece dated July 26, 1882, proves that the work was ongoing at this time: "On account of building and repairing the school house, the Sunday-school is held at Miss Eliza Benedict's villa on every Sunday afternoon at half-past four."

An excellent thesis paper entitled "A History of Schools in Bethel, Connecticut" written by Bethel teacher Eleanor C. Coffey in 1969 contains a good deal of relevant information on the Plumtrees School. About this particular time period she states:

> *By 1884, the attendance had so increased, approximately 62 pupils, that it became necessary to build an addition. The building was adorned by a cupola, the work of Legrand Street, and a large bell, donated by James Barnum, was installed. It became a two-room school, primary and upper grades. But after a few years trial, the two rooms proved impractical, and the partition was removed, making one large room.*

Although the date of 1884 is used here rather than 1882, it is unquestionably the same renovation and expansion previously described. The year 1884 may denote the final completion of long-range building improvement project. A close examination of the current building reveals that the addition was placed at the west end of the school, facing Taylor Road. Differences in the foundation masonry, telltale seams in the roof's overhang and an exposed support beam in the interior's ceiling all clearly indicate this. A measurement of the building shows that its width is 22 feet, 4 inches and that its original length was exactly 32 feet. The new addition extended the building precisely 10 feet to the west for a new total length of 42 feet. This added roughly 205 square feet of new classroom space. It is conjectured that each of the two windows that had previously been on the west wall of the school were then repositioned, one on each side of the building. To maintain symmetry and balance, the other side windows may also have been shifted in position. The school's ornate cupola and its distinctive three-panel pointed arch window and octagon-shaped gable end window would have been added at this time as well. Both the cupola and large west end window share the same architectural style that is today referred to as Carpenter Gothic. Legrand Street, the individual credited with doing the work, lived nearby and is shown as being twenty-four years old and working with his father, Alonzo, in a carpenter's shop in the 1880 U.S. census. Two years later, he may have been attempting to demonstrate the proficiency of his skills in his work on the school's renovation.

In 1888, ownership of the school was officially transferred from the Plumtrees School District to the town of Bethel as part of a larger school consolidation. In the next few years, the town's population would rise slowly and reach just over 3,000 inhabitants by 1890 (3,401). It would then essentially level off with the exception of a minor dip between 1890 and 1900, with the loss of 74 inhabitants, and a larger one between 1910 and 1920, with a decrease of 591 citizens. By 1940, the town's population had broken 4,000 residents (4,105), and by 1950, the 5,000 mark had been passed (5,104). But within the next twenty years the town would increase its population more than it had in the last 150, adding a staggering 3,096 residents in the 1950s and another 2,745 in the 1960s. This time period witnessed the closing of all of Bethel's other one-room schoolhouses in Grassy Plain (1895), Wolfpits (1918), Elmwood (1928) and Stony Hill (1941). The Plumtrees School now stood alone as the last of a dying breed. The little white school weathered all of these storms of growth and change, but not without help, and not without some controversy as well.

On July 19, 1939, an organization calling itself the Plumtrees School Association was established. Made up of the parents of children attending the school, the primary goal of the association was to supplement the facility's town funding, which was proving increasingly inadequate. The association began its activities in September 1939 after obtaining $100 in donations from the people of the school district. Association meetings were held at the school every second Thursday of the month, and all residents of Plumtrees were welcome to attend. Among the initial items provided by the group were "pencil sharpeners, first aid kits, globes and telephone service," as well as making necessary repairs to the building itself. During this time period, the building's clapboard siding was covered with shake shingles. A dental fund was also established for students whose families could not afford dental care on their own. Later, similar funds were set up for vaccinations and doctor's visits. Other purchases included "a motion picture projector, and films, playground equipment and a radio." A set of encyclopedias, as well as newspaper and magazine subscriptions, was also supplied. In 1940, forty-eight chairs and a piano were purchased. In a surviving annual report of the association dating from June 1956, mention is made of the school's new heating system: "Alas, the little white schoolhouse no longer has the 'pot-bellied' stove standing up front. Gone are the days when wet mittens dried out on its shield. But also gone are the days when it constantly had to be tended to." At some point between 1953 and 1955, a new entrance was created at the northwest corner of the building, presumably to make it easier for students to board the school buses that were now in greater use.

The group sponsored annual Halloween and Christmas parties, as well as school picnics that were always well attended. Men involved in the association met on Sundays to repair the building and improve the schoolyard, and the group purchased a sign to serve as an honor roll for former students who had served their country in war. The Plumtrees Association raised its funds through such varied activities as "auctions, lawn parties and a harvest game social held in the fall." There were also barn dances, "card parties, harvest bingos, skating parties and strawberry shortcake suppers." An article published in the *Danbury News-Times* at the time the group disbanded explained, "The old-fashioned lawn parties were famous in the area, annually packing into the school grounds 300 to 400 persons. A feature of the day before the affair was the driving of a horse and buggy around Bethel as an advertisement."

In December 1951, the Plumtrees School Association purchased land that adjoined the school directly to the east. The land was to be used as additional play area and picnic grounds. The lot was approximately 360 feet long and cost $600 plus legal fees. When the association disbanded, the property was transferred to the Bethel Lions Club with two stipulations: 1) that it never be built upon and 2) that the Bethel Boy Scouts would always have use of the land for their activities. This land was later turned over to the Town of Bethel, keeping the two provisos in place.

The Plumtrees School Association lasted for exactly thirty years, ceasing activity in July 1969. Its demise was brought about by the changing nature of the school's student population. Seven grades were taught at the school as late as 1950, but as the district's population increased, class size did likewise.

In order to accommodate the larger classes, the number of classes served was decreased. In 1950, the number of classes served was decreased from seven to five. In 1954, the number was reduced to four; by the end of the 1956–57 school year, it was reduced further to three, serving the first, second and third grades. When the school opened in September 1957, it served only one class of third graders. In 1962, the school switched to serving only kindergarten students drawn from all parts of the town, with one session being held in the morning and another in the afternoon. This switch was made following a sizeable controversy that centered on facilities at the school that some parents perceived as antiquated and unhealthy.

On September 11, 1957, a petition was presented to the Bethel Board of Education by twenty-one parents and guardians of sixteen students from the Stony Hill district who were attending the Plumtrees School. The petition cited the "unsanitary and unsafe conditions of the outhouse, the lack of washing facilities and the inadequate lighting." (The "washing facilities" at this time amounted to a container of cleansing cream positioned on top of the upright piano and paper towels. The only water source came from the hand-pumped well located a few yards from the building.) The petitioners requested that their children "be transferred to one of the extra classrooms at Berry School." (Berry School at that time was in the process of completing a new addition that made provisions for the town's projected population growth.) On October 23, the Board of Education approved the request of the parents and announced that the Plumtrees School would close the following day, bringing to an end its ninety-year history. However, the transfer of the thirty-one students affected failed to take place.

On October 25, the Board of Education announced that it had decided to delay the transfer after a public outcry and a counter-petition presented by the Plumtrees School Association that bore the signatures of 136 citizens. By December, despite an offer by the association to finance the cost of updates to the building if no other form of financing was available, the Board of Education voted to uphold its original decision. The school closed for its Christmas vacation, and upon reopening in January, its 31 students were relocated to the extra classroom space at Berry School. The Plumtrees Schoolhouse would find itself without students for the next five years. During this time, many people worried that due to Eliza Benedict's original 1867 proviso, the town might lose ownership of the property owing

An October 25, 1957 *Danbury News-Times* photo showing students leaving the Plumtrees Schoolhouse at the end of the school day. A little over two months later, the old school was closed, and the same students pictured here were transferred to Berry School due to parent complaints regarding the one-room schoolhouse's lack of indoor plumbing. The school would reopen in 1962, with plumbing, and serve as a kindergarten until June 1970. The teacher shown in the photo is Miss Edith Cushnie.

to the fact that it was not being used for school purposes. Luckily, that situation never arose, but the fear of this possibility would reappear more than a dozen years later.

On August 22, 1962 a *Danbury News-Times* article announced "Plumtrees School to Open Again." The decision to reopen the school had been announced at a Board of Education meeting held two days earlier on Monday, August 20. The board decided to reopen the school after being faced with growing enrollments and finding that upgrading the old school would cost less than renting an alternate facility. The article goes on to herald the changes that had been made since the school's last use:

A new toilet has been built into the rear of the back hallway. Pipes have been installed from the drinking fountain, to the well which many area residents still visit because of its excellent drinking water. A new ceiling has been installed in the classroom. The walls have been renovated and painted a soft green. Blackboards line the walls of the room. The windows, which had been boarded up for years, have been opened, brightening the room considerably.

In a true test of its dedication, the Plumtrees School Association had remained in operation even during the school's closure, maintaining and protecting the school and still providing scholarships and services to the students of the district. Upon hearing of the plans to reopen the school, the association's members were jubilant and announced that they would reinstall playground equipment that had been purchased and then stored away while the school was not in operation.

The school continued to serve as a kindergarten with morning and afternoon sessions, each serving approximately twenty-five to thirty students until 1970. In February of that year, the Bethel Board of Education's business manager, Robert S. Bullard, issued a report that suggested "that for financial and staff reasons," the Plumtrees School should be closed. Citing such concerns as the uneconomical use of a teacher's aide, who would ordinarily serve a larger number of students, sending a custodian once a day to clean, and having school buses routed by the school four times a day specifically for only two classes brought about costs that could be eliminated by closing the school and having the kindergarten classes transferred to other schools. In commenting on the recommendation, Bullard added the personal suggestion that the school be designated as a historical site. In June 1970, the little white schoolhouse said goodbye to its last students. A century of educational service had come to an end. Once again, the specter of having the property reclaimed by the heirs of Eliza Benedict was raised and fretted about, only to have nothing come of it.

An effort by Edward J. Gallagher, president of the Bethel Historical Association, to have the school officially declared a landmark never gained traction, and when that organization itself became defunct in the time following the school's closing, the effort was abandoned. The building still saw some service on Thursday evenings, as it was used by the forty Boy

Scouts who made up Bethel's Troop 167. On November 23, 1972, the Bethel Visiting Nurse Association made a request of the Board of Education to be allowed to use the building for a newly formed well-child clinic program. It stipulated that it would renovate the building in a way that would not damage its historic interior or make it unusable by other groups. The Board of Education granted the request, and on March 24, 1973, the clinic opened. The *Danbury News-Times* article of the following day noted:

> *Splintered floor boards have been replaced by blue soft carpet. The once paint-chipped walls are now paneled and decorated with bright paintings. Instead of old, initialed-carved desks with ink stains, shiny new medical equipment waits for a time when the schoolhouse will once again be filled with children. Only a set of swings and see-saw in the front yard is a reminder of Plumtrees School's past.*

The VNA well-child clinic would continue to use the school on a limited basis for the next thirty-three years. By 2006, the Visiting Nurses Association had acquired other space for its clinic and no longer saw a need to use the building. Its fate was once again in jeopardy. Once more, people wondered whether Bethel might lose its title to the property. But just like the cavalry riding to the rescue in an old western movie, a new reincarnation of the Plumtrees School Association was formed and asked permission of the town's board of selectmen to restore the old school to its former glory. It hoped to again use the school for educational purposes by making it available for Bethel's elementary students to visit, so that they might acquire a firsthand experience of school life in the nineteenth century.

The request was granted, and within the next year, the new association was successful in having the building placed on the state of Connecticut's Register of Historic Places. The group's members then removed the paneling that had been placed over the old blackboards in 1973, located a replacement bell and restored it to its place in the cupola, obtained school desks of the period and positioned them just as others had been placed so many years before, returned the exterior color to white after over a quarter of a century of it being red and, in short, did everything possible to return the school to its appearance of earlier days. At the time of this writing, the school looks better than it has in many decades, and its preservation seems ensured for a good time to come. Somewhere, Miss Eliza Benedict must be smiling.

No account of the Plumtrees Schoolhouse would be complete without mention of a woman who taught an estimated twelve hundred students there between September 1916 and June 1957: Mrs. Anna H. Rockwell. Mrs. Rockwell was born Anna H. Ruffles on November 24, 1890, in the Palestine district of Newtown to Mr. and Mrs. Walter and Jane Ruffles. She graduated from the Palestine District School and from Newtown High School. Following her graduation from high school, she taught for four years at the Palestine School before entering the Danbury Normal School, completing a two-year course of study in only one year, graduating in the spring of 1916. She began teaching at the Plumtrees School the following autumn. In 1920, she married Frank G. Rockwell, who was a farmer by trade but also served as the Plumtrees School custodian beginning in 1920 and later acted as a traffic officer as well. Mrs. Rockwell was a much-beloved teacher who took her position very seriously and was never late to school a single day. Residents often said, "You can set your watch by her." She tolerated no nonsense in the classroom but was so well liked that most students were seldom disruptive. After teaching for four decades in the one-room schoolhouse, Mrs. Rockwell announced that she would retire at the end of the 1956–57 school year. In tribute to her long career, she was the recipient of a testimonial dinner held on December 5, 1956, at the Avalon Inn, in Stony Hill. The event was attended by 150 guests, many of whom were her former pupils.

On March 15, 1971, Anna Rockwell was again recognized for her many years of service by having a new elementary school named in her honor. She accepted the tribute with the same grace and humility she had always displayed. Mrs. Rockwell spent most of the next three years at her home on Rockwell Road before dying at the age of eighty-three on March 18, 1974, at the Glen Hill Convalescent Center in Danbury. She was fondly remembered as a teacher who had made a lasting impression on her students, and many of them still recall her fondly today, not only for her method of instruction but also for her kindness and strength of character.

Other teachers who have taught at the Plumtrees School have included Mary H. Fairchild, Edith Cushnie, Helen Chapman, and a teacher who retired in 1878 and was identified only as Miss Selleck.

16

Bethel's Most Familiar Symbol
"The Spirit of the American Doughboy"

T he statue stands at the center of Bethel's town green and has become the community's most familiar symbol; the majority of townspeople simply refer to it as "the Doughboy." In reality the statue's true title is *The Spirit of the American Doughboy*, and its history is worthy of note.

Even before the Barnum Fountain's bronze figure of a triton was carted away in October 1923, the people of Bethel knew that they would need to find some type of substitute for the popular attraction that had served as the town's centerpiece for over four decades. Most citizens agreed on the idea of honoring the Bethel veterans of World War I. Some suggested leaving the fountain basin in place and placing a concrete pillar or piece of native stone emblazoned with a bronze plaque in its center where the figure of the triton had once stood and then re-plumbing the fountain jets to supply a spray that would shower the monument at intervals. An article in the *Danbury Evening News* from October 18, 1923, mentioned that a suitably large boulder could be found near the residence of Lyman Whitehead on Codfish Hill Road. The unnamed citizen who suggested this approach stated that "it would be possible to move it to the park in the center of the village during the winter season by placing it on skids and moving it when the ground is coated with ice and snow." In addition, the plan's proponent "said he wished that three sturdy oak trees might be procured from the native woods and set up in the park as a memorial to the three young men of Bethel who gave up their lives for their country in the recent world conflict."

The idea of utilizing a native stone was not entirely popular with everyone. Joseph Vaghi, a local cabinetmaker and proprietor of the Bethel Rustic Work Company submitted an editorial to the Danbury paper in which he stated:

> *A large stone as nature formed it, may be all right in some places and for some purposes, but its appearance at best is crude and cold. In it would not be seen the handiwork of man, or anything that was artistic, or pleasing to the eye, and future generations would probably condemn us as being too lazy to create things, and indifferent to anything ornamental or beautifying.*

The question of what type of monument to create dragged on for months, and at a town meeting held on April 16, 1924, a motion was made and passed that "a memorial not to be combined with a fountain be secured and that the fountain be demolished." However, due to disagreements on just what type of memorial to create and how to best to pay for it, Bethel's town green would go without a centerpiece for the next four years. In the end, a unique plan was devised to make the memorial a reality.

A group called the Community Association had previously initiated an effort to buy a building at 82 Greenwood Avenue that had briefly served as a church hall for the Congregational Church. The association sold shares for the buying of the hall with the intention of having it serve as a community house that "when paid for would be turned over to the town as a memorial to the boys who served in the World war." In the end, the building was sold by the association to the Masons for use as a Masonic Temple, and these proceeds were then used to purchase the memorial. This is the explanation for the large inscription on the statue's base that reads, "Erected By The Community Association of Bethel in Honor of Her War Veterans."

By May 1928, all was in readiness for the dedication of the new memorial. The *Danbury Evening News* reported that "plans are progressing well for the observance of Memorial Day, and the dedication of the bronze statue, that will be erected in the Fountain park as a memorial to war veterans." It was further stated that a short parade would take place before the unveiling of the statue that would include within its ranks a Connecticut National Guard artillery unit, surviving Civil War veterans (riding in automobiles), Spanish-American War veterans, the Veterans of Foreign Wars, the American Legion and the Boy Scouts. The article also related that "the foundation for the statue base, was completed at the Fountain park to-day, and as soon as it has hardened, the granite base, which has been cut by M.H. Schlitter of Danbury, will be placed in position. The bronze statue, which will top the granite base arrived in Bethel about two weeks ago, and was stored until needed."

Memorial Day, Wednesday, May 30, 1928, the day set for the dedication of the new statue, was marred by rain. The Danbury paper reported that "a majority of those gathered about the statue, were unprepared for rain and, while some remained, many scattered and went home before Sergeant Barlow (the principal speaker of the day) had finished his appropriate address." Approximately 179 men from Bethel saw service in the Great War, and the day's proceedings were particularly poignant for those who remembered the three young men from Bethel who had died serving their country. Again, the Danbury paper tells the details:

> The first to make the "supreme sacrifice" was the first boy who enlisted, James Masson, who entered the service as a member of a regimental band organized in Newark, N.J. He died in a camp in the south. The other boys were James H. Trowbridge, who answered the first local appeal for volunteers, entering the U.S. Marines. He served overseas in some of the principal battles and was reported "missing" in the closing battle of the war. Henry Bromley was the third man to lose his life, going into service as a member of the 56th C.A.C. (Coastal Artillery Guard) of Danbury.

All three of these soldiers are buried in the Center Cemetery on South Street. James H. Trowbridge's nephew and namesake was given the honor of unveiling the statue.

The new statue was described in the following manner:

> The statue is of bronze, representing an American doughboy poised ready for action in full combat equipment, holding aloft a hand grenade in his right hand, while a rifle is held in his other hand at his side. He is shown standing in front of a torndown barbed-wire fence. The figure is of cast bronze heavily reinforced and seven feet in height. It stands on a Vermont gray granite base and the whole statue thirteen feet, four inches in height. On the front of the base is the inscription cut into the stone, and is plainly

A 1932 postcard view of *The Spirit of the American Doughboy* statue located in what was then still referred to as Fountain Place. The statue was designed by the artist E.M. Viquesney, and copies of the work can be found in thirty-nine of the fifty states.

readable from the street in passing. The granite base is five feet square at the base and three feet at the base of the die, while the statue base is two feet square.

E.M. Viquesney (pronounced Vick-KAY-nee) was the artist who created and marketed the statue, and his name is inscribed at the rear of its base. Today, there are approximately 140 known examples of this same statue distributed throughout thirty-nine of the fifty states. Connecticut has two: the one in Bethel and another in North Canaan. The style of the statue found in Bethel was created from bronze sheets and is in actuality six feet, eight inches high, and its base is three feet, eight inches wide.

The sculptor, whose full name was Ernest Moore Viquesney, was born on August 5, 1876, and died on October 4, 1946. He was a native of Spencer, Indiana, lived there most of his life and committed suicide shortly after the death of his second wife. Viquesney was highly successful in marketing his statue, and multiple examples can be found in nearby states. Massachusetts has one in Winchendon. New York locations are Vestal, Castile and Harrison. New Jersey's statues are found at Belmar, Dover, Fair Haven, Frenchtown, Matawan, Perth Amboy, Roselle Park and Secaucus. Vermont's "Doughboys" are in Enosburg Falls and St. Albans.

There is one additional story that proves the Doughboy statue has not always been universally appreciated. In the early 1930s, Bethel was home to Art Young, one of America's foremost political cartoonists and an avowed socialist. He lived on Chestnut Ridge Road and treasured his rural retreat in what was then a very small New England town. It appears that Young was greatly upset when the Doughboy statue was erected and very much lamented the loss of the famous Barnum fountain that had preceded it. In a book he entitled *Art Young: His Life and Times*, the cartoonist lambasted Bethel for its selection of the World War I memorial. He wrote:

> *I think it sad that the village selectman one day around 1920* [actually 1923] *had the fountain demolished. They said it was cracking and sold it to a junk dealer. Then what? In its stead they erected one of those libels on American youth, a big bronze male out to kill—typical statue in American towns to commemorate the "war for democracy."*

Young stated that such memorials were "jokes" and were "insulting to anyone with a sense of the artistic."

Despite Young's venomous diatribe, the statue has come to be cherished by our townspeople, reminding of us of our veterans and serving as the centerpiece for our Memorial Day, Veteran's Day and Fourth of July celebrations, just to name a few. And although the Bethel statue has been damaged on more than one occasion, either by falling tree limbs or climbing teenagers, the town has always diligently made repairs, and subsequently the statue still proudly stands as the focal point of P.T. Barnum Square, which, incidentally, many people still refer to as "Doughboy Square."

17

Barnum's Fabulous Fountain

I t was raining in Bethel on the morning of August 19, 1881. But no degree of precipitation could dampen the spirits of the town's inhabitants on that day. Homes and stores were decorated with flags. Columns and posts were wrapped with bunting of red, white and blue at every turn. A parade was to be held that would include fire companies and their engines, marching bands and citizens of prominence riding in shiny black carriages. The entire town was abuzz with the anticipation of seeing their most famous prodigy return in triumph, and he was presenting a gift as well. Phineas Taylor Barnum, the world's greatest showman and Bethel's native son, was set to arrive for the unveiling of a fabulous fountain that would now grace the town square. Despite the rain, thousands would gather in the center of the ordinarily sleepy village to witness his arrival, to hear him speak from a specially constructed platform and, above all, to take in a close-up view of the community's new centerpiece.

The subject of all the attention was born in Bethel on July 5, 1810, in a home situated on what was then called Elm Street (today's 55 Greenwood Avenue). Beginning in 1816, he attended a small one-room schoolhouse just a few hundred feet west of his family home. He later attended the Danbury Academy, walking three miles to and from its doors six days each week. He unwillingly did chores on his family's farmland, clerked in his father's store and later assisted in the running of his parents' tavern. In truth, the

An image of Fountain Place, or present-day P.T. Barnum Square, as it looked in a postcard dating from 1906.

young Barnum spent a good deal of his time listening to the fanciful yarns of Bethel's seemingly unlimited supply of "characters" and practical jokers, the foremost member of this group being Barnum's own maternal grandfather, for whom he was named, Phineas Taylor.

As he grew older and was compelled to struggle for his own support, Barnum's views on work changed. Although he still shunned hard physical labor, he readily embraced economic endeavors that promised to quickly improve his financial standing. He opened his own store, became a lottery agent and initiated Bethel's first newspaper, the *Herald of Freedom*. He became a master of the chicanery and double-dealing that he had witnessed at his grandfather's knee. He coupled this with a shameless form of ballyhoo that made his more puritanical townspeople blush, yet still view him as someone who would go far. He married a local girl named Charity Hallett when he was only nineteen and the following year had a house built at what is now 44 Chestnut Street. The couple occupied the home until the winter of 1834–35 when they left so that he might seek his fortune in New York City. Within ten years, his name would be known throughout the country and on both sides of the Atlantic. He had decided on the career of showman, exhibiting rare and unusual acts and exhibits to an increasingly comfortable middle class. In rapid succession, he presented such astounding wonders as Joice Heth, the supposed nurse maid of George Washington, "the Feejee Mermaid," General Tom Thumb, the Swedish opera sensation Jenny Lind, Eng and Chang the original Siamese twins, Jumbo the elephant and, over the years, a multitude of others. He opened a series of museums to house his wonders, and each of them became essential tourist attractions in the cities in which they were found. Most notably, he had associated himself with the form of entertainment for which he would best be remembered: the great American circus. Just a year before this visit, Barnum had entered into a business association with James A. Bailey. Later, in a different incarnation of this association, Barnum & Bailey's Circus would be heralded as "the Greatest Show on Earth." In addition to all of these business endeavors, Barnum had found time to serve as mayor of Bridgeport and as a state representative in the Connecticut General Assembly. Over the course of his long career, he had also developed friendships and acquaintances with kings, queens, presidents and literary figures. He was said to possibly be the most famous man in the world. Such was the stature of the man who arrived in Bethel on that rainy August day.

The primary purpose of Barnum's visit was to bestow on his birthplace a token of his affection. As Barnum would later write, he presented his gift "desiring to aid in beautifying the village of Bethel it being my birthplace, from which a busy checkered life has never alienated my interest." In true showmanship fashion, he presented a gift the likes of which the people of Bethel had never seen before. The story behind the gift is one that demonstrates Barnum at his best.

On one of his many trips to Europe, Barnum had purchased a bronze fountain for the reported cost of $10,000 (over $220,000 in today's terms) in Berlin, Germany. The fountain was shipped back to America and installed on the grounds of his magnificent Bridgeport estate called Waldemere. The grounds of Waldemere were open to the public and attracted a great many visitors. However, judging by subtle innuendos made in the Danbury newspapers, the large fountain may have required a greater amount of water than anticipated and, while providing a spectacular display, might also have produced water pressure problems in Barnum's residence. Either out of sincere generosity or sheer necessity, Barnum decided to approach the city officials of Bridgeport with the offer of donating the fountain to his adopted home. When these leaders dawdled in providing a clear response, Barnum was apparently miffed and turned instead to the town of his birth. Bethel's officials were more responsive to the offer, and an agreement confirming the acceptance of the fountain was reached between Barnum and town fathers of Bethel on May 15, 1881. (The town's government might have been forced to decline had it not implemented a municipal water system flowing from the Eureka Reservoir only two years previous.) In this agreement, Barnum promised to transport the fountain to Bethel and put it in running order at his own expense. Now the only remaining problem was where to put it.

Even before the debate began about where best to place the fountain, some of the shrewd Yankees from whom the young Barnum had learned his craft voiced the opinion that they were not quite convinced that they were getting a good bargain. The *Danbury News* of May 25, 1881, expressed their views: "Careful Bethelites figure that the expense of the ground for the location of the fountain and then putting it in appropriate condition will cost several thousand dollars." The article, however, goes on to counter this view with the thought that "Bethel will never again get so favorable a start in the way of ornamentation as this fountain will give, and it should have a park any way." It seems the naysayers were eventually won over.

In deciding upon the best site for the new fountain, townspeople were divided. Some favored placing it on the hill behind Nehemiah B. Corning's residence at what is today's 120 Greenwood Avenue. Others argued for placing the fountain in what was known as "Miss Seelye's Grove." This land today is the open area on the eastern side of the Bethel Public Library at 137 Greenwood Avenue. "Miss Seelye" was Miss Hannah H. Seelye, who occupied the nearby house at that time. (In her will, Hannah H. Seelye would leave the house and grounds to the town for use as a public library.) A third group favored creating a new town square at the intersection of Wooster Street and Center Street (now Greenwood Avenue). This approach would require obtaining land from both Oscar H. Hibbard, who owned land on the west corner of Wooster Street, and William C. Shepard who owned the land on the eastern corner. In the end, this third plan was the one that was formally adopted.

The *Danbury News* announced on June 22 that "at last, the location of the fountain has been settled, and work has begun." The paper went on to say:

Mr. Brothwell, Mr. Barnum's agent, was in town Tuesday, and staked out the ground for the basin of the fountain and work will be begun right away. (Charles R. Brothwell was employed by Barnum to oversee his many real estate properties.) The stone for the copings are being gotten out in New Haven, and as soon as the basin is ready the fountain will be brought to Bethel and set up. It has already been loaded on the wagon ready to start for its new home.

By July 16, the *Danbury Democrat* was able to report, "A neat marble slab bearing the following inscription, 'This fountain presented to the Borough of Bethel by Hon. P.T. Barnum, May 15th 1881' has been placed in the foundation wall of the fountain. The work progresses finely and will soon be completed." A few days later, the same paper suggested that Bethel "purchase four lamps and place them around the fountain. It will add to its beauty day and night." This suggestion would later be implemented.

At first, the dedication day was announced for Wednesday, August 17, but was then quickly switched to Friday, August 19. A general holiday was declared, and Bethelites were encouraged to turn out in force as a way of expressing their gratitude for Barnum's munificence. On August 16, citizens were informed not only that Barnum would provide the fountain but also that he had supplied an additional $700 for purchasing the required land for its placement and having it graded and that he had decided to supply a drinking fountain as well. The *Danbury Democrat* would later point out one added expense for Barnum. "One of the horses that started out from Bridgeport to draw the wagon which contained the fountain was taken sick on the road and died." The writer of the news items then rather impishly added, "This was perhaps an item of cost not considered by Hon. P.T.; but he can stand it."

At the stroke of twelve on the appointed day of August 19, the grand parade for Barnum began in spite of rain-filled skies and wound its way throughout the town's mud-covered principal streets. Upon arrival at the newly created square, two brass bands performed, and once their playing ceased, Barnum gave the command that the fountain should be unveiled. Ten young girls of Bethel who were specially selected for the occasion were given the honor of performing the unveiling, which was accomplished "amid cheers from the multitude and national airs by the bands."

The sight that Bethelites first beheld that day was undoubtedly a wonder to the eyes. Sprays of water shot forth from a fountain that stood eighteen feet high, filtering down to a basin that was fifty-two feet in diameter. In the basin's center stood the figure of a triton, or merman, blowing a conch shell, perched atop four large sea shells that were in turn balanced on the tailfins of four dolphins. The triton's conch shell erupted in a blast of liquid that spouted far into the air above, in four different streams at once, with the resulting contents gently cascading down to create four small pools of water in each of the large shells below. Meanwhile, the four dolphins, as well as the base below them, sent out jets of white water with tremendous force, flooding the huge basin that surrounded them. The figure of the triton faced in a southwesterly direction as if he were looking down Center Street,

This circa 1910 postcard view of the Barnum Fountain provides great detail. The fountain was purchased by P.T. Barnum in Berlin, Germany, and was based on one completed in 1643 by the Italian sculptor Gian Lorenzo Bernini that still stands in the Piazza Barberini in Rome.

and the marble dedication stone bearing Barnum's name was placed in the basin's outer wall facing the same way.

Although not mentioned that day, the oversized ornament that Barnum had obtained in Berlin was a bronze interpretation of a famous Italian landmark. This Teutonic work of artistry was clearly based on Baroque sculptor Gian Lorenzo Bernini's Fontana del Tritone completed in 1643. This fountain is in the Piazza Barberini in Rome, and a photographic comparison with the Barnum fountain shows that the similarities are undeniable. Also not mentioned was the fact that in its original setting at Barnum's Waldemere, the statue sat on a large base that sported the initials "PTB' in enormous letters. (A wonderful photograph of the fountain in its initial setting can be found on page 276 of a book entitled *P.T. Barnum, America's Greatest Showman* produced in 1995 by Philip B. Kunhardt Jr., Philip B. Kunhardt III and Peter W. Kunhardt.)

Following the formal unveiling, Barnum took center stage and delivered an impromptu speech that ran on at great length and spilled over with memories of his days in Bethel, placing an emphasis on how far American culture had progressed from the primitive days of his youth. He had been seriously ill in the months preceding the event, but now he was recovered and showed no signs of diminished capacities as he called to mind from memory no fewer than the names of 152 Bethel citizens from his earlier days and shared humorous anecdotes relating to many of them. For most in the audience that included many of his childhood friends, now in their seventies like Barnum himself, the most touching and sincere lines came at the outset of the address when he declared, "My Friends: Among all the varied scenes of an active and eventful life, crowded with strange incidents of struggle and excitement, of joy and sorrow, taking me often through foreign lands and bringing me face to face with the king in his palace and the peasant in his turf-covered hut, I have invariably cherished with the most affectionate remembrance the place of my birth." Later, when his verbal memoir had run its course, he expressed his desire to see many of the cherished parts of Bethel that possessed "euphonious" names such as Wolfpits, Stony Hill, Plumtrees, etc., and of course his "noble, blessed, historical Ivy Island."

There were other speakers, poets and presentations that followed, but none could the match the excitement of seeing and hearing "the great Barnum,"

Fountain Place, or today's P.T. Barnum Square, as it looked circa 1906. The large hat factory shown at the left burned in 1913. The buildings at the right, all dating from 1894, still survive.

and as the ceremonies wound down, the crowd began to slowly diminish. The weather was taking its toll, and much of the food and refreshment that had been set out on tables was spoiled by the drenching rain.

In the days following the fountain's dedication, a steady stream of visitors flowed into Bethel to see the remarkable attraction. The most frequently asked question on everyone's lips was, "Have you seen the fountain?" The square that had been created for Barnum's gift was eventually labeled Fountain Park, and the street on either side of the green was christened Fountain Place. It became *the* place in Bethel to be photographed, and later, with the creation of postcards, the fountain became their most popular subject.

As with so many things, as time passed the fountain was taken for granted. The small fence that encircled the basin was composed of vertical wooden posts, painted white, which supported horizontal iron poles. The fence began to be damaged by visitors, primarily children, presumably sitting on them as if they were benches, attempting to balance themselves on them like they were high-wire acrobats or, worse yet, jumping up and down on them until the poles began to bend. Sometime around the turn of the century, this small barrier was removed. The drinking fountain that stood on the green's south end, only a few steps from the edge of Center Street, was another early casualty. Within a few short years after its installation, it ceased to function and was not repaired. Instead, it was made into a decorative planter. Later, when a trolley line was created, it seems that a widening of Center Street necessitated that the former drinking fountain, now planter, be moved to the north side of the fountain's park. Ironically, this cast-iron decorative element may be the sole surviving vestige of anything associated with Barnum's fountain, as it is believed to be the same planter that can now be found on the west side of the Bethel Public Library, featured as the centerpiece of a Shakespeare garden. (Perhaps this is appropriate, as Barnum was often referred to as the "Shakespeare of Advertising.")

Most damaging to the fountain was the practice of allowing it to remain running throughout the winter until it became encapsulated in multiple layers of ice. Although the frozen fountain presented an image pleasing to the eye, it also did untold damage to its inner workings, which, over time, would require constant repair. Eventually, this damage would cause the fountain to

A 1920 postcard showing the famous Barnum Fountain presented to Bethel by the great showman in 1881. By October 1923, the fountain was judged to be an outdated eyesore and was dismantled and sold for scrap. Note the planter behind the fountain. It is believed to be the same one that now stands in a Shakespeare garden on the west side of the Bethel Public Library.

be permanently shut off. On August 4, 1923, the town's board of selectmen inspected the fountain and rendered the verdict that even attempting repair was unsafe, based on the fear that parts of the triton figure might break off and injure anyone venturing to fix its damaged components. They therefore recommended its removal. On October 18, 1923, the *Danbury Evening News* carried this sad message: "The last remains of the statue presented to the town by the late P.T. Barnum were carted away this morning by the workmen who yesterday tore it down and smashed it into pieces. Only the stone base support and the huge basin remain to mark the spot where for so many years the Barnum fountain stood." That week the *Bridgeport Post* carried a photograph of the remains of the broken figure of the triton lying in a pile of rubbish at a salvage yard in Danbury. The bronze figure was later sold to a New York foundry that melted it down for its metal. At a town meeting held on April 17, 1924, the citizens present voted to have the fountain's basin demolished as well.

Years later, on June 5, 1949, the *New York Herald Tribune* ran a story about the fountain. The article featured a photograph of Bethel Police chief Morris S. Britto posing with the marble dedication slab that had once adorned the

This 1920s postcard shows the Barnum Fountain and a view looking west along Greenwood Avenue.

This view of Fountain Place, or present-day P.T. Barnum Square, dates from about 1906 and shows the famous Triton Fountain bequeathed to Bethel by P.T. Barnum in 1881. Directly behind the fountain can be seen one of Bethel's largest hat factories, which was for many years operated by the firm of Cole and Ambler.

fountain's foundation wall. Since 1948, the marble stone has also been lost to history; its whereabouts are unknown. The square where the fountain stood maintained the name Fountain Place until 1960, when it was officially changed to "P.T. Barnum Square." For years afterward, a small establishment at the northeast corner of the square retained the name Fountain Liquor Store before adopting a new one. Now, very little is left to remind us of the elaborate gift that Barnum once gave to the people of Bethel, in his words, "as a small evidence of the love which I bear them and the respect which I feel for my successors, the present and future citizens of my native village."

18
Barnum's Last Visit to Bethel

U ndoubtedly, Bethel's most famous prodigy is P.T. Barnum. Barnum is most remembered for the founding of his circus, dubbed "the Greatest Show on Earth," but he made perhaps an even greater impact on history with his innovations in advertising and promotions. Barnum, it seems, could sell anything to anybody and often did. Even to a public fully conscious that it was being "humbugged," Barnum's name came to symbolize the unusual, the bizarre and things that were bigger than life.

One of Barnum's promotions that certainly was bigger than life was the tremendous pachyderm named Jumbo. Standing at twelve feet high and weighing seven tons, Jumbo was the wonder of the 1880s. Today, the term jumbo-sized has come to indicate anything extraordinarily large; witness jumbo jets, jumbo shrimp, etc. Other terms and phrases such as Siamese twins or describing something as a white elephant can be traced to Barnum. In his eighty years, the great showman flimflammed and bamboozled thousands and won and lost a fortune several times. The one thing he never achieved was anonymity. At the time of his death, Barnum was considered one of the best-known personalities on the planet.

Barnum's life began in Bethel on July 5, 1810, and ended in Bridgeport on April 7, 1891. Even though well over a century has passed since Barnum's death, many of the places Barnum would have known are still with us. Barnum's birthplace, although radically altered after a fire in the 1840s, still stands at 55 Greenwood Avenue in a form that he would still certainly recognize. The tavern, which was run by Barnum's father, Philo, from 1819 until his death in 1826 and later by his mother until 1835, still stands at 4 Chestnut Street. The house Barnum had specially built for himself and his new bride, Charity Hallett, in 1831 is now home to the Sandbox Nursery School at 44 Chestnut Street. Ivy Island, the celebrated piece of real estate bequeathed to Barnum by his grandfather as a practical joke, which the showman later used as collateral when purchasing his American Museum, still exists at the end of an access way leading from Walnut Hill Road to a Northeast Utilities Power Station near the rear of the Bennett property. His father, Philo Barnum, who died on September 7, 1826, has his grave in the old burying ground located next to the Congregational church on Main Street. His mother, Irena Taylor Barnum, who died on March 14, 1868, is buried in Center Cemetery on South Street. Both parents can be found among scores of others who all share a genealogical connection to Bethel's most famous citizen. Barnum's first major attraction, Joice Heth, is also interred in the old burying ground on Main Street, but the location of her grave is unknown.

A circa 1910 view of the Irena Barnum Homestead at 55 Greenwood Avenue. P.T. Barnum was born in an earlier house that stood on the same site. After a newer house was built in 1843, his mother, who had moved elsewhere, purchased the family's old property and lived here until her death in 1868.

The following newspaper account comes from the August 8, 1889 issue of the *Danbury Evening News* and describes P.T. Barnum's last visit to Bethel at the age of seventy-nine, less than two years before his death. It is presented here in its complete and original form. (Note: The residence of I.H. Wilson mentioned in the account is today's 4 Chestnut Street.)

BARNUM AT BETHEL
Visiting the Scenes of His Childhood Days
(From our Bethel Correspondent)

Bethel was honored with distinguished guests yesterday. A man known the world wide and whose name is familiar with all. P.T. Barnum expressed a desire some weeks ago to visit his birthplace once more, perhaps for the last time, and before he sailed for Europe. Arrangements were made for his coming several times but the stormy weather made a postponement necessary on each occasion. Thursday was finally selected and proved to be a beautiful day for his visit.

A native townsman with the fame of Barnum would naturally attract a good deal of attention, and the great showman's coming was looked forward to by many with interest. Mr. Barnum was accompanied by his sister, Mrs. Amerman, who resides at Brooklyn, N.Y., and his eldest daughter, Mrs. D.W. Thompson. The party arrived on the 10:13 express. They were met at the depot by a reception committee, composed of some of Bethel's oldest citizens, who escorted the visitors to the residence of I.H. Wilson, on Chestnut Street. Barnum's carriage was followed by a long string of carriages containing citizens, making quite a procession, and when they reached Mr. Wilson's, people thronged about the distinguished visitors and cheered them loudly.

The welcome address was made by E. Romine Barnum, in a most pleasing manner. It was ably delivered and at times he was quite eloquent. More appropriate remarks could not have been made. At the close of his speech the veteran showman quickly responded. He is the same old Barnum. Age does not drive away a particle of his love for fun, and he believes in enjoying yourself while you can, at least he said so. He stood there hat in hand, his bald head glistening in the sun, which is surrounded by a wreath of hair white with age and very curly. His remarks were brief, and in opening expressed his great surprise and delight in meeting with such a hearty welcome. Although a native of Bethel, at the present day he was probably better acquainted with more people in the city of London than he was in his native town. He was glad to see many familiar faces, a few of whom were his schoolmates in his youthful days. Others had passed away. This should not be a vale of tears, said Mr. Barnum, but all should try and enjoy themselves. We are all one family and should have no enemies. I haven't an enemy in the world, said Mr. Barnum, that I know of. In closing he once more thanked the people for so nice a reception and hoped to be able to meet them again.

Hand shaking occupied several minutes after Barnum's remarks, and it was great sport to witness the introduction of the many old men to Mr. Barnum. When he came to one of his old school mates he was like a colt let loose in a five acre lot, so great was his delight.

The party were driven about town before and after dinner, which was elaborately served at Mr. Wilson's. He visited many scenes of his childhood days, among others, his once famous Ivy Island. For, said Barnum as he entered his carriage for the drive, "Above all things let me see Ivy Island." The visitors left town on the 3:47 train, the greatest showman of the age feeling that he had been fully paid for his visit to his native town.

A 1908 postcard view of Bethel's center as seen from Hoyt's Hill. The house that P.T. Barnum had built at 44 Chestnut Street in 1831 and occupied until early 1835 can be seen in white, in the foreground of the old Center School.

Just as he had sensed, this was to be Barnum's final time in the town of his birth. Upon his death on April 7, 1891, the *Danbury News* commented, "The success of P.T. Barnum may be considered phenomenal. It is estimated that during his 50 years of show life, 100 million people have visited his various attractions. Genial, open and free hearted to a fault, the name of P.T. Barnum will live on for many generations." And so it has. Barnum is buried in the Mountain Grove Cemetery in Bridgeport along with his first wife, Charity Hallett. Their graves are only a short distance from that of the Prince of Humbug's greatest protégé, Charles S. Stratton, otherwise known as "General Tom Thumb."

Bibliography

Bailey, James M., and Susan Benedict Hill. *History of Danbury, Conn., 1684–1896*. Bowie, MD: Heritage, 1998.

Barber, John W. *Historical Collections of Connecticut*. New Haven, CT: [s.n.], 1836.

Barber, John Warner, Christopher P. Bickford and J. Bard McNulty. *John Warner Barber's Views of Connecticut Towns 1834–36*. Connecticut: Acorn Club, 1990.

Barnum, Phineas Taylor. *The Life of P.T. Barnum Written by Himself*. Urbana: University of Illinois, 2000.

Barnum, Phineas Taylor, and Arthur H. Saxon. *Selected Letters of P.T. Barnum*. New York: Columbia University Press, 1983.

Barnum, Phineas Taylor, and Waldo R. Browne. *Barnum's Own Story; the Autobiography of P.T. Barnum, Combined & Condensed from the Various Editions Published during His Lifetime*. Gloucester, MA: P. Smith, 1972.

Benedict, Henry Marvin. *Bethel Connecticut Centennial 1855–1955*. New Haven, CT: Columbia Printing Company, 1955.

———. *The Genealogy of the Benedicts in America*. Albany, NY: J. Munsell, 1870.

Betts, Henry B. *List of Houses Hundred Years Old or Over, Standing February 1921 in the Vicinity of Danbury, Connecticut*. Photostat. Connecticut State Library, 1921. Print.

The Book of Trades, or Library of Useful Arts. Part III. Illustrated, with twenty copper-plates. 1st American ed. Philadelphia: for Jacob Johnson, 1807.

Coffey, Eleanor C. *A History of the Schools in Bethel, Connecticut*. Master's thesis. Western Connecticut State University Archives, 1969.

Commemorative Biographical Record of Fairfield County, Connecticut, Containing Biographical Sketches of Prominent and Representative Citizens, and of Many of the Early Settled Families. Chicago: J.H. Beers, 1899.

Connecticut; a Guide to Its Roads, Lore, and People. Boston: Houghton Mifflin, 1938.

The Connecticut Guide: What to See and Where to Find It. A Project of the State Planning Board Initiated under CWA and Completed with FERA Funds. Hartford, CT: Emergency Relief Commission, 1935.

Crofut, Florence S. Marcy. *Guide to the History and the Historic Sites of Connecticut*. New Haven, CT: Yale University Press, 1937.

Dexter, Franklin Bowditch. *Biographical Sketches of the Graduates of Yale College with Annals of the College History*. New York: H. Holt, 1885.

The E.M. Viquesney "Spirit of the American Doughboy" Database. "Sculptor E.M. Viquesney and His Creations." http://doughboysearcher.weebly.com.

FamilySearch.org. Free Family History and Genealogy Records. http://www.familysearch.com.

Gallagher, Edward J. *History of Bethel, Connecticut: An Excerpt from Plan of Development, Bethel, Connecticut*. New Haven, CT: Technical Planning Associates, 1969. Print.

Goodsell, Lewis. *A History of Bethel, Connecticut, 1759–1966: A Commemorative Book*. Bethel Historical Society and Bicentennial Commission, 1976.

———. *Two Hundred Years of the First Congregational Church, Bethel, Connecticut*. N.p.: L. Goodsell, 1976.

Hickok, Charles Nelson. *The Hickok Genealogy; Descendants of William Hickocks of Farmington, Connecticut, with Ancestry of Charles Nelson Hickok*. Rutland, VT: Tuttle Pub., 1938.

Hurd, D. Hamilton. *History of Fairfield County, Connecticut: with Illustrations and Biographical Sketches of Its Prominent Men and Pioneers*. La Crosse, WI: Brookhaven, 2007.

Judd, Sylvester. *Thomas Judd and His Descendants*. Northampton, MA: J&L Metcalf, 1856.

Kunhardt, Philip B., Philip B. Kunhardt and Peter W. Kunhardt. *P.T. Barnum: America's Greatest Showman*. New York: Knopf, 1995.

McPherson, Hannah Elizabeth (Weir*)*. *The Holcombes, Nation Builders: Their Biographies, Genealogies, and Pedigrees*. Salem, MA, n.d.

Saxon, A.H. *P.T. Barnum: The Legend and the Man.* New York: Columbia University Press, 1989.

Shepard, Gerald Faulkner. *The Shepard Families of New England.* Vol. 2. New Haven, CT: New Haven Colony Historical Society, 1972.

Starr, Burgis Pratt. *A History of the Starr Family: of New England, from the Ancestor, Dr. Comfort Starr, of Ashford, County of Kent, England, Who Emigrated to Boston, Massachusetts, in 1635; Containing the Names of 6766 of His Descendants, and the Record and History of 1794 Families.* Hartford, CT: Case, Lockwood and Brainard, 1879.

Van Dusen, Albert E. *Connecticut.* New York: Random House, 1961.

Walters, Judith Allison. *Remembering Plumtrees: A Personal Look Back at Bethel, Connecticut.* N.p.: privately published, 1997.

Wood, Frederic J., and Ronald Dale. Karr. *The Turnpikes of New England.* Pepperell, MA.: Branch Line Pr., 1919,1997. Print.

About the Author

Patrick Tierney Wild is a Bethel native who has served as the town's municipal historian since 1993. He attended kindergarten at the Plumtrees one-room schoolhouse, went to St. Mary's Elementary School and Bethel High School and has a BS degree from Rutgers University and an MA from the College of New Rochelle. He has written articles for the *Danbury News-Times*, *Bethel Home News* and *Bethel Beacon* and has provided historical information for biographical documentaries on P.T. Barnum for both the Arts & Entertainment Channel and the Discovery Channel. He is the author of *Images of America: Bethel*, a photographic history. He served as a Bethel selectman from 2003 to 2007. He is employed as a social studies teacher at Ridgefield High School, where he teaches advanced placement courses in both United States history and United States government and politics.

Visit us at
www.historypress.net